Revolution
IN THE
Andes

TRANSLATED BY DAVID FRYE

FOREWORD BY CHARLES F. WALKER

A Book in the Series

LATIN AMERICA IN TRANSLATION / EN TRADUCCIÓN / EM TRADUÇÃO

Sponsored by the Duke–University of North Carolina Program in Latin American Studies

SERGIO SERULNIKOV

Revolution
IN THE
Andes

....

The Age of Túpac Amaru

Duke University Press Durham and London 2013

© 2013 Duke University Press
All rights reserved

Printed in the United States of America on acid-free paper ∞
Designed by Courtney Leigh Baker and typeset in Quadraat
by Keystone Typesetting, Inc.

Library of Congress Cataloging-in-Publication Data
Serulnikov, Sergio.
[Revolución en los Andes. English]
Revolution in the Andes : the age of Túpac Amaru / Sergio Serulnikov ;
translated by David Frye ; foreword by Charles F. Walker.
pages cm — (Latin America in translation/en traducción/em tradução)
Includes bibliographical references and index.
ISBN 978-0-8223-5483-3 (cloth : alk. paper)
ISBN 978-0-8223-5498-7 (pbk. : alk. paper)
1. Peru—History—Insurrection of Tupac Amaru, 1780–1781.
2. Tupac-Amaru, José Gabriel, –1781. 3. Bolivia—History—To 1809.
I. Title. II. Series: Latin America in translation/en traducción/em tradução.
F3444.S47513 2013
980'.01—dc23
2013012814

For my daughters Irina and Maia

CONTENTS

FOREWORD

Sergio Serulnikov has written the best overview in Spanish—and now in English—of the fascinating and influential Túpac Amaru and Katarista uprisings that stormed through Peru and Upper Peru (today's Bolivia) in the early 1780s. Rebellions led and backed by native Andean people (Quechua and Aymara) took control of much of the area that stretches from the Inca capital of Cusco to the Potosí mines. Insurgents rampaged through the countryside, sacked haciendas and mills, occupied small towns, and sieged the largest cities, Cusco and La Paz. Weak colonial militias crumpled almost immediately, forcing the Spanish to rely on troops from distant Lima and Buenos Aires. The rebels controlled much of this core Andean area, putting into place alternative forms of political rule and social order. The non-Indian population feared for their lives; authorities in Lima, Buenos Aires, and Madrid worried that they could lose control of the Peruvian Viceroyalty. The Túpac Amaru and Katarista rebellions were the largest in colonial Spanish American history.

It is not a simple story. With his sharp eye for comparisons and his fine pen, Serulnikov highlights the differences between the different phases or locations. The Túpac Amaru rebellion, based in the area between Cusco and Lake Titicaca, was unusual in that it had a single leader, José Gabriel Condorcanqui. An ethnic authority or *cacique* as well as a merchant, Condorcanqui moved easily between Indian and Spanish society. He had assumed the name Túpac Amaru II to stress his Inca bloodlines.[1] Túpac Amaru called for a return to Inca rule and claimed to fight in the name of all oppressed Peruvians—Indians, mestizos, blacks, and even some Europeans, whether born in the Old or New World. While he and his influential wife, Micaela Bastidas, preached the need for a multiracial and multiclass alliance that respected the Catholic Church, his Indian followers showed much less sympathy toward creoles (people of European descent born in the Americas) and Spaniards, whom they understood as their exploiters and enemies. Túpac Amaru and Micaela Bastidas demanded tolerance; rebel forces frequently ignored them and killed anyone considered a European. They also, in some cases, targeted priests and attacked churches. Despite these internal differences, however, the movement remained cohesive. Even after Túpac Amaru and Bastidas's executions, his son and cousin took the lead and continued to fight in his name.[2]

On the other side of Lake Titicaca, the uprisings varied greatly in social composition and tactics. The Katarista movement was actually a series of unique revolts and military campaigns. In Chayanta, north of Potosí, a humble Indian, Tomás Katari, led Indians' efforts in the late 1770s to rid themselves of a cacique and to ease the heavy tax and labor demands on Indians. The nonviolent struggle stalemated, and Katari took the case to the courts in Buenos Aires. Tensions and aggression escalated, and what had first been a negotiation and then a court battle became a violent revolt. Serulnikov underlines how these events developed within the colonial fold. The growing frustration of Katari and the people he represented brought to light the contradictions and strains of Spanish rule in the Andes. The denouement was not pleasant: among the leading figures, rebels beheaded a cacique, Indians slaughtered a corregidor and tore his eyes out, and authorities killed Katari by throwing him off a steep cliff.

1. Túpac Amaru I (1545–1572) led the final stages of the Inca resistance against the Spanish in Vilcambamba. The Spanish captured him in the jungle and beheaded him in Cusco.

2. Serulnikov provides an excellent bibliography. I will cite only some key works in English. For English-language documents on these rebellions, see Ward Stavig and Ella Schmidt, eds. and trans., *The Tupac Amaru and Katarista Rebellions: An Anthology of Sources* (Indianapolis: Hackett, 2008). See also the essays in Stern 1987 and Stavig 1999. I am finishing a narrative history of the Túpac Amaru uprising to be published by Harvard University Press in 2013.

Chayanta was one of several battlegrounds. Rebels in and around the city of Oruro, seeking a broad coalition, aligned with creoles, who resented the favoritism toward European-born Spaniards. This horrified local Spaniards. Elsewhere, after Tomás Katari's death, his brothers, Dámaso and Nicolás, took the struggle beyond Chayanta, toward Chuquisaca, forming a mass rebel army that swept through towns and communities. In 1781, a humble Indian, Julián Apaza, who took the name Túpac Katari to invoke the two major rebel factions, assailed Spanish forces in the area between Lake Titicaca and La Paz. He led two sieges of La Paz that stretched for more than one hundred days, some of the most gruesome moments of the uprising. More than ten thousand residents died of hunger, dehydration, and disease, while survivors scrounged desperately for food. In mid-1781, with the Katari brothers and Túpac Amaru and Micaela Bastidas already dead, the Túpac Katari and Túpac Amaru uprisings overlapped in La Paz and sought to align. A broad Andean coalition, the prospect of which had haunted colonial authorities since the initial disturbances, seemed imminent. It did not materialize.[3]

Serulnikov tells these stories well, clarifying the main events and capturing vivid moments. While portraying each of these movements in its own light, he points out intriguing differences and parallels and probes the largely failed efforts to coordinate. He pays particular attention to various forms and understandings of violence. He not only shows the brutality of both the rebels and the royalists, but also looks at the use of humiliation (authorities forced to dress as Indians before their execution) and the acts of desperation in the sieges of La Paz (reported cannibalism among the starving). He also probes obvious questions overlooked by most historians. For example, at the same time that he depicts the intimidating power of the rebel guerrilla forces, he draws attention to the essential advantage held by the colonial forces due to their firepower, labeling the struggle "a clash between stones and guns." Serulnikov also notes how little is known about the thousands of Indians who fought for the Spanish.

In the introduction, the author outlines different generations of his-

3. Notable studies in English include Thomson 2002; Robins 2002; and Serulnikov 2003.

torians' views on the uprisings. These rebellions have been the subject of dozens or even hundreds of monographs, and both Túpac Amaru and the Kataristas have a colossal presence in the understanding and representation of the past in Peru and Bolivia. Their role in the national imaginations cannot be underestimated. He divides the studies into three categories: older works that stressed the importance of the rebellions, underlined their impact in the wars of independence from 1808 to 1825, and uncovered important sources; publications in recent decades that look at the structural causes of the insurgency, essentially the economic pressures and political changes prompted by the Bourbon Reforms in the latter half of the eighteenth century; and those scholars who have examined Inca nativism or utopianism.[4]

Serulnikov seeks to refocus the debate. Building on these studies, he calls for a political analysis, one that scrutinizes what the rebels sought, both the leaders and the followers. Following his pathbreaking book on the Kataristas (particularly the Chayanta phase), *Subverting Colonial Authority*, he contends that the different revolts all evolved from within the colonial system (Serulnikov 2003). They were not nihilist outbreaks or the desperate acts of the disenfranchised. Instead, authorities such as corregidores and the courts lost legitimacy over time as Indians' efforts to ward off the reforms and defend traditional rights stalled or failed. This prompted Indians to take up arms, in an act they believed acceptable within Spanish political culture. This argument about the need to focus on politics, in my mind, is both an important contribution and a welcome redirection of the historiography. Serulnikov builds respectfully and intelligently from decades of research by historians and much discussion about the significance of the Andean rebellions.

Some readers, however, might want to understand how historians have answered the key question: why did they rebel? These three schools of thought or generations, particularly the political and economic explanations dating from the 1970s, deserve a bit of review. In essence, scholars showed the impact of the changes implemented by King Charles III (1716–1788, r. 1759–1788), especially the widespread disgruntlement

4. Particularly significant was O'Phelan Godoy 1985. See also Fisher, Kuethe, and McFarlane 1990.

throughout Spanish America regarding the reforms. Immersed in endless wars in Europe and cognizant that its hold on its American possessions was fragile, Spain decreased the percentage of American-born authorities, tightened the bureaucracy, and ultimately increased the tax burden on just about everyone. Caciques such as Túpac Amaru were squeezed from below and above. They lost local support as they oversaw the collection of ever-higher taxes yet also had to struggle to maintain their position, because the Bourbons understood ethnic caciques as an unfortunate remnant of the past. In the latter half of the eighteenth century, the reformers challenged indigenous communities' political autonomy. Moreover, while taxes increased, traditional forms of exploitation such as the mita labor draft for mines, especially Potosí, continued to weigh heavily on Andean people. Nonetheless, as Alberto Flores Galindo argued, the Bourbon Reforms were the context rather than the cause of the eighteenth-century uprisings (Flores Galindo 2010 [1987]: 84–86, 112–113). Therefore, to understand why the rebellions erupted when and how they did, scholars such as Serulnikov have examined local political currents, without losing sight of broader ideological changes and adaptations.

Serulnikov's range as an historian and skills as a writer come out clearly in this magnificent synthesis. *Revolution in the Andes* leaves no doubt that any serious analysis must look at local conditions. Simply put, the makeup of community politics, the root of these outbursts, and the ensuing political fault lines varied greatly across the Andes (Serulnikov 2003; Thomson 2002). The author brings to life the growing tensions in Chayanta and beyond prompted by the increased demands on Indians and the breakdown of the older "colonial pact."[5] He also illuminates the renaissance of Inca nationalism in Cusco and the fragile alliances in Oruro. Yet, while giving each of these movements or spaces their due, he also compares them brilliantly, highlighting parallels and contrasts. This book's readability—due in part to the fine work of the translator, David Frye—should not mask the fact that it is a deeply analytical work, one that builds on generations of scholarship on "social movements" (a rather sanitized-sounding term preferred by many scholars), legitimacy, and power.

5. Tristan Platt developed the notion of a colonial or tributary pact. See Platt 1982: 40.

Sergio Serulnikov is a gifted writer. He combines gory yet telling anecdotes about chopped-off heads or dogs eaten by the starving in La Paz with clear summaries and even a bit of humor. While well written and captivating, the book builds on a massive amount of research by other scholars and the author's ability to think and rethink, compare, and summarize. Serulnikov has produced the best narrative history of the violence that swept the Andes in the early 1780s.

Charles F. Walker
University of California, Davis
June 2012

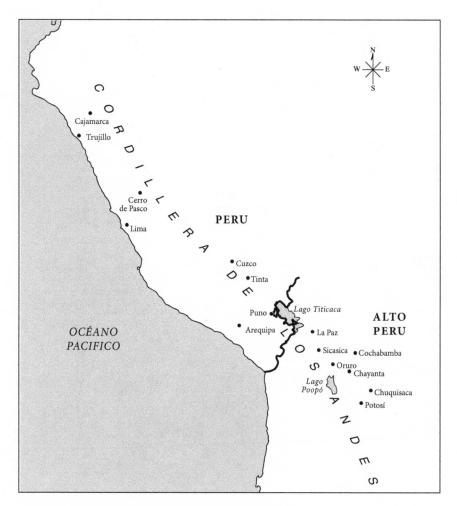

Peru and Upper Peru (Bolivia)

Provinces in the regions of Northern Potosi and La Paz, Upper Peru (Bolivia)

Provinces in the regions of Cuzco and the Collao, southern Peru

1

....

The Violence of Facts

No event shook the foundations of the colonial order in Spanish America more profoundly than the massive uprising of the Andean peoples in the early 1780s. Over the course of more than two years, whole insurgent armies were organized, from Cusco in southern Peru all the way south to territories that now belong to Chile and Argentina. Some of the oldest and most populous cities in this region—Cusco, Arequipa, and Puno in southern Peru; La Paz, Oruro, and Chuquisaca (today Sucre) in Upper Peru (modern Bolivia)—were besieged, assaulted, or occupied. Huge swaths of countryside in the jurisdiction of Charcas, in the highlands surrounding La Paz, and in southern Peru fell under the full control of the rebel forces. At times those forces attracted explicit support, or tacit sympathy, from large numbers of mestizos and creoles living in rural towns and urban centers.[1]

The conflagration took place in the very heart of the Spanish empire in South America: an extensive economic zone that stretched along the

1. In Spanish America, creoles or *criollos* were people born in America who traced their descent from Spain and identified culturally with Spain. Mestizos were people of mixed ancestry.

route linking Lima to Buenos Aires. At its hub was Potosí, one of the world's greatest sources of silver, the main export commodity of the Americas and the engine of regional development. The insurgency also encompassed other mining towns, such as Puno and Oruro; fertile agricultural lands, including Cochabamba, Arequipa, Ollantaytambo, the Yungas, and Abancay, that supplied the Andean cities with grains, sugar, coca leaves, wine, and brandy; rich cattle-raising areas like Azángaro province; and textile mill zones, such as the provinces of Quispicanchis and Canas y Canchis near Cusco. These large territories were mainly inhabited by Aymara- and Quechua-speaking peoples, the descendants of the great pre-Columbian polities: the Charka-Karakara confederations in the southern Andes; the Aymara kingdoms of the Collao, the region around Lake Titicaca; and, of course, the mighty Inca empire, which by the time of the European invasion had expanded from its core in Cusco to dominate the entire Andean region. Though many of the Indians who joined the uprising worked permanently in the mines, cities, and Spanish haciendas, the vast majority belonged to native communities that owned the land collectively and maintained their own governing structures, including the *caciques* (indigenous ruling elites) and other lesser ethnic authorities. From these rural groups the Spanish treasury drew its most dependable source of fiscal revenues, the Indian tribute, and the mining industry its most dependable source of labor, the mita—a colonial institution that forced each Andean community in the area to send each year to Potosí and other mining towns one-seventh of their population. Members of the indigenous communities were the heart and soul of the insurrection.

By virtue of their sheer magnitude the uprisings completely overwhelmed local militias. Regiments of the regular army had to be sent in from the distant viceregal capitals, Lima and Buenos Aires. In Cusco alone, more than seventeen thousand soldiers were mobilized against the Túpac Amaru forces. The Crown had not been compelled to mobilize its armies since the distant days of the conquest, when the Pizarro and Almagro families tore each other to bits over the right to control the newly discovered territories and populations. It is difficult to establish the precise number of casualties. Some sources estimate that about a hundred thousand Indians and some ten thousand persons of Hispanic origin—Peninsulars (Spaniards from Spain itself), creoles, and mestizos (people of mixed ancestry)—died over the course of the conflict. Although the numbers are imprecise, it is clear that in a society with a population of no more than a million and a half, the death rate was appalling.

Like any major revolutionary movement, this uprising occasioned the rise of charismatic figures whose names reverberated across the continent, and even beyond. They left behind vivid and powerful myths that pervaded—and still do pervade, with unfaltering intensity—the historical consciousness and political imaginaries of the Andean peoples: José Gabriel Condorcanqui, a cacique from Canas y Canchis province in southern Peru, who took the name Túpac Amaru II to signal his kinship with Túpac Amaru I, the last Inca emperor executed in 1572 in Cusco by orders of Viceroy Francisco de Toledo; Tomás Katari, an Indian peasant from northern Potosí who became the symbol of resistance to colonial rulers in the Charcas region; and Julián Apaza, a petty merchant from an indigenous village in Sicasica province who led the siege of the city of La Paz and called himself Túpac Katari to symbolize the intimate linkages between the events taking place southward and northward of the La Paz region.

Behind these men and these events one can discern the outlines of an idea—an idea diffuse and malleable enough to harbor disparate and at times contradictory expectations, but one whose essential message nobody should have missed: a demand that the government of the Andes be restored to the land's ancient owners.

2

....

The Violence of Time

The French historian and philosopher Ernest Renan famously declared that "forgetting, and getting one's history wrong, are essential factors in the making of a nation" (Renan 1995 [1882]: 145). A key moment in the history of the Andean societies, the dramatic events of 1780, has taken on many different incarnations over time. In the formative years of the countries that emerged from the dissolution of the Spanish empire, these events were consigned to oblivion or reduced to an isolated, albeit spectacular, episode in the decline of the colonial regime. How could the massacres of men, women, and children who had taken refuge in churches, or the devastating siege of La Paz and other cities, be reconciled with the self-proclaimed march of progress and the embracing of European paradigms of social and political development? How could the subjugation of the Indians to the new republican elites be reconciled with the grand monarchical aspirations of Túpac Amaru and his hundreds of thousands of followers?

To be sure, the Peruvian and Bolivian upper classes were not blind to the cultural heritage of the populations they ruled. Inca civilization was occasionally appended to the genealogical tree of the nations. Influential figures such as Andrés de Santa Cruz, president of the failed Peru-Bolivian

Confederation of 1836–1839, and his obstinate enemy, the powerful Cusco caudillo Agustín Gamarra, made the first efforts in this direction. Yet exalting the virtues of the Andeans of the past did not prevent them from condemning the backwardness of Andeans in the present, and thus justifying the forced labor regimes or the condition of legal inferiority that continued to weigh them down just as in the time of the viceroys. "Incas yes, Indians no" is the maxim that best seems to encapsulate the spirit of the era.[1] The Tupamarista revolution was too radical, and too recent, to be domesticated, stripped of its disquieting anticolonial connotations, folklorized, processed by the collective memory of the new nation-states.

It would take more than a century for the year 1780 to cease being a date in the history of savagism and become a date in the history of the nation. By the mid-twentieth century, the conjunction of sweeping political changes, the unraveling of vigorous popular movements, and the growing influence of indigenista and Marxist intellectuals of various creeds contributed to the birth of a new narrative. With the rise to power of populist and reformist coalitions—the Nationalist Revolutionary Movement in Bolivia in 1952, and General Juan Velasco Alvarado in Peru in 1968—there were attempts to recognize Quechuas and Aymaras as full citizens, agrarian reforms were implemented, and the Peruvian and Bolivian governments forged close alliances with working-class unions and peasant organizations. In this new climate of ideas, Túpac Amaru found a new home. The Andean leader now appeared as the embodiment of resistance by the people—all the people, not just the Indians—to colonial oppression. His figure took on the dimensions of a founding father; his cause, that of an epic patriotic saga. The publication of a multivolume collection of documents on the Tupamarista rebellion in the early 1970s by Peru's military government stands as a monument to this ideological endeavor.[2]

Scholars also participated in this process of reinvention. In the 1940s and 1950s, Polish-Argentine historian Boleslao Lewin, Bolivian historian

1. Cecilia Méndez (1995) uses this slogan as the title of her study of creole nationalism in Peru. See also Walker 1999 and Aljovín de Losada 2005. (The translation of this title phrase and all translations from Spanish sources in the present book are by David Frye, except for citations from works published in English translation.)
2. See the ten volumes of *Colección documental de la independencia del Perú* (1971).

Jorge Cornejo Bouroncle, and Peruvian historian Daniel Valcárcel wrote the first professional studies on the topic. Based on painstaking archival research, their works offered an account of the events that would not be revised for many years to come. The overarching interpretative frame of these narratives is encapsulated in the very titles of their books: *The Túpac Amaru Revolution: Forerunner to Independence from Colonial Rule* (Cornejo Bouroncle); *The Túpac Amaru Rebellion and the Origins of American Independence* (Lewin); and *Túpac Amaru, Forerunner to Independence* (Valcárcel) (Cornejo Bouroncle 1949; Lewin 1957; Valcárcel 1977). This loud chorus underlines the widespread belief of the era in the close bonds that presumably existed between the indigenous insurrection of 1780 and the creole independence movement thirty year afterward. Now taking the form of a marble statue, Túpac Amaru seemed to look down in satisfaction from his pedestals in the city plazas onto his new seat of honor in the country's pantheon of heroes. So said the state, and so said the historians.

This interpretation proved ephemeral, however. There is no question that Túpac Amaru (though not necessarily his peers to the south of Lake Titicaca) appealed to notions of American or Peruvian patriotism in his formal declarations, or that some Hispanic groups, resentful of the direction that Spanish rule had been taking since the mid-eighteenth century, initially favored the insurrection. Some creoles even took on leadership roles in it. But soon enough, it became evident that the social antagonisms the rebellion had unleashed were as damaging to the Españoles Americanos (the creoles) as to the Españoles Europeos (the Peninsulars). The deep anticolonial stance of the movement was not so much geopolitical as ethnic and cultural. It also had a definite class component. In the eyes of the peasant masses, including many of their leaders, the distinction between Peninsulars and creoles was utterly irrelevant. In addition, the mobilization of thousands of Indians, whatever their overt aims, inevitably tended through its own dynamics to dismantle the established forms of authority, economic control, and social deference. It does not take a historian or social scientist to understand this. At the outset of another of the great social cataclysms in Latin American history, the 1910 Mexican revolution, the dictator Porfirio Díaz, a very old hand at interpreting these matters, berated his enlightened opponents for believing that the uncontainable destructive force of a social revolution could be restrained by virtuous government programs and statements of good intentions. Before going into exile, he remarked that Francisco Madero had "unleashed the tiger" in his zeal to transform Mexico into a liberal democracy. "Now let's see if he can control it," he famously added. The ten years that followed, which shook the country to its core and changed the course of its history forever, answered this query. Much like Porfirio Díaz, but 130 years earlier, the creole landowners, merchants, mine owners, lawyers, and state officials—the future leaders of the young Andean nations—realized that the return of the Inca did not augur well for them. How could it?

By the 1970s and 1980s, therefore, the Tupamarista revolution had acquired a new image and a new destiny. Earlier generations had characterized the movement as a prefiguration of the creole cause; now they began to define it by what made it different. That is, the events of 1780 could be explained only by the existence of a unique Andean worldview. At the center of that worldview was a cyclical concept of time, which foretold the return of past civilizations and conceptualized historical change as the result of larger cosmological changes. Historians now argued that the rebellion had been preceded by the spread of prophecies, myths, and miracles announcing the changing of an era, a *pachakuti*, which would put an end to the dominion of the Spaniards and their gods. The Incas would rule again in this world; the Andean deities, in the other one. The Amarus and Kataris were seen not merely as charismatic leaders but as bearers of divine powers, the prophets of a new era. The pan-Andean uprising suddenly ceased to evoke the subsequent revolutions for national independence, with their vague beliefs in the virtues of the French Enlightenment and Anglo-Saxon liberalism, and began instead to be linked to a different order of phenomena: the millenarian, messianic, and nativist movements that punctuate the history of the lower classes in medieval and early modern Europe, as well as the anticolonial resistance movements of Asia and Africa. What inspired the native peoples to rise up in arms was not emancipation from Spain but a utopian ideal: their projection into the future of an idealized golden age from the past. And that utopian ideal was distinctively Andean. *In Search of an Inca: Identity and Utopia in the Andes* is the title the finest Peruvian historian of the era, Alberto Flores Galindo, chose for his book on the topic. Another Peruvian historian, Manuel Burga, and the Polish historian and anthropologist Jan Szeminski entitled their books *The Birth of a Utopia: The Death and Resurrection of the Incas* and *The Tupamarista Utopia*, respectively. Other times, other choruses (Flores Galindo 2010 [1987]; Burga 2005 [1988]; Szeminski 1984).[3]

The studies of the 1970s and 1980s on the Andean utopia were largely in line with contemporary trends in the field of history at large, such as the growing influence of the history of mentalities and structural anthropology. They would not have been possible without the remarkable surge of Andean ethnohistory, a discipline that approaches the indigenous societies of the past with the questions, methods, and contributions of the ethnography. It is hard to overstate the impact, both direct and indirect, of the ethnohistorical works of John Murra, Tom Zuidema, Franklin Pease, and Nathan Wachtel, to name only a few, on the analysis of these events (Murra 1975; Wachtel 1976; Pease 1973; Zuidema 1990).[4] But the climate of ideas in which these studies prospered was even more extensive and profound. It was the same climate of ideas that led, in Bolivia, to the formation of the first "Katarista" indigenous organizations and unions, a name that by itself signals a search for an ideological and cultural identity separate from the traditional Marxist groups and the country's most powerful political party for most of the twentieth century, the Revolutionary Nationalist Movement. The fundamental antagonism underlying contemporary Bolivian society could not be reduced to class struggle or populist nationalism; it was an ethnic, colonial conflict born the very day Christopher Columbus caught sight, without knowing it, of a new continent. Túpac Katari embodied this conflict as no one else did. The discourse of Evo Morales, and the ideological outlook of the social movements that brought him to national prominence and in 2006 elected him the first indigenous president in Bolivian history, are incomprehensible outside of this deep shift in the way power relationships in the Andean world are conceived. In Peru, for its part, studies of the Andean utopia coincided with developments that would long dominate the political agenda of the country and the front pages of newspapers around the world: the rise of the Shining Path (Sendero Luminoso) and the Túpac

3. Other important works on this topic include Hidalgo Lehuede 1983 and Campbell 1987.

4. See also the essays in Ossio 1973.

Amaru Revolutionary Movement. It should not be surprising, then, that by the mid-1980s, as the tragic consequences of revolutionary armed struggle became apparent, a new generation of Peruvian historians accused their predecessors of reifying Andean culture and endowing indigenous peoples with an essentialistic atavism that they neither possessed nor desired—not at the close of the twentieth century, and not at the end of the eighteenth.[5]

But beyond this complex intertwinement of history and politics, a consensus began to emerge among scholars: far from prefiguring independence, the Tupamarista uprising was one of the reasons that emancipation from Spain had to be forced upon Peru and Bolivia by the arrival of José de San Martín's and Simon Bolívar's revolutionary armies (which does not deny that certain sectors of the population played active roles in the process), was late in coming (Peru and Bolivia were the last two countries on the Spanish American mainland to declare independence), and was profoundly conservative (aimed at preserving rather than transforming the colonial social hierarchies). Fear of a new 1780 was a factor, but not the only factor, in this outcome. The image of Túpac Amaru as an enlightened harbinger of the new Andean republics had run its course. Few have seemed interested in reviving it since then.

In his poem "The Heights of Macchu Picchu," standing before the overwhelming spectacle of temples and craggy peaks, Pablo Neruda wondered: "Stone upon stone, and man, where was he? / Air upon air, and man, where was he? / Time upon time, and man, where was he?" (Neruda 1991 [1950]: 38).[6] By the early 1990s, scholars interested in this other astounding spectacle, the great Tupamarista rebellion, could ask similar questions. After nearly half a century of research, conferences, and symposia, not much was known about the motives that had driven hundreds of thousands of Indians to risk everything. It is true that in the 1970s and 1980s, in parallel and often in dialogue with the works on the Andean utopia, extensive socioeconomic research made it possible to discern some of the main grievances behind the rebellion: rising taxes, commercial monopolies, demographic pressure, and the increasing ille-

5. Examples of critical analyses of essentialist constructions of Andean identities and worldviews include Estenssoro Fuchs 2003; Méndez 2001; and Ramos 1992.
6. "Macchu Picchu" is Neruda's idiosyncratic spelling of Machu Picchu.

gitimacy of their ethnic chiefs. Drawing to varying degrees on the quantitative methods and *longue durée* focus of the French *Annales* school, on Marxist-inspired British social history, and, more distantly and critically, on the earlier literature on the transition from feudalism to capitalism, dependence theory, and the modes of production in Latin America, these studies did much to avert simplistic depictions of the pan-Andean uprising as an isolated response to generic colonial exploitation. The Tupamarista revolution was indeed the corollary of long-term cycles of social protests associated with specific changes in the living conditions of the Indian population and other sectors of colonial society. The social composition and structure of the movement's leadership during its different phases seemed to reflect the economic tensions that lay behind its outbreak. Key works in this vein include *Túpac Amaru II—1780*, edited by Flores Galindo; *Repartos y rebeliones: Túpac Amaru y las contradicciones de la economía colonial*, by Jürgen Golte; and especially *Rebellions and Revolts in Eighteenth Century Peru and Upper Peru*, by Scarlett O'Phelan Godoy (Flores Galindo 1976; Golte 1980; O'Phelan Godoy 1985).[7]

In the end, nonetheless, socioeconomic tensions tell us little about how the insurgents imagined the new order of things or why they acted in the ways they did. This is particularly true for a historical phenomenon of this magnitude, reaching far through time and space, varied in its social makeup, and complex in its modes of collective action and ideological outlooks. As mentioned above, there were also clues about the mental structure of the Andean peoples: their conceptions of time, the meanings they attributed to the Incan imperial tradition, their religious beliefs. But mental structures are a poor substitute for economic reductionism. In the first place, the range of beliefs and expectations during the course of the disturbances cannot be reduced to a few common traits. Not everyone rebelled because they were waiting for a new Inca. And those who did expected very different things from the new Inca. More generally, systems of cultural beliefs, much like socioeconomic structures, can only provide the context for experience, not experience

7. On rebellions in the Quito region, see Moreno Yáñez 1977. Some of the most influential books on eighteenth-century regional and economic history include Glave and Remy 1983; Larson 1988; Moreno Cebrián 1977; Sánchez-Albornoz 1978; and Tandeter 1992.

itself. To reconstruct the social experience, we have to restore its meaning. And to restore the meaning of the Tupamarista experience, we must do nothing less than recover the political dimension of the event, thinking of the place of the Andean peoples and their leaders not as somewhat passive agents of large economic trends and systems of thought, but as what they really were: political actors. Only in this way can the vast archival remains of Spanish colonialism help us answer the question that the imposing monumental ruins of the Incan civilization refused to provide the Chilean poet: "and man, where was he?"

It took a new research agenda to understand this process. It called for discerning how native peoples interacted with government institutions, articulated their own notions of justice, and endeavored to establish mechanisms of solidarity and mobilization that would counter persistent tendencies toward fragmentation. It was necessary to look past their grievances and examine the political culture that enabled them to translate their discontent into collective mobilization. Common wisdom today holds that memory—what humans believe they recall—is a construction, that memory is political. But the opposite is equally true: memory is the stuff politics is made of. There is no politics without memory. Today we take this collective memory for granted: it is always there, political parties and social movements stir it up, social scientists scrutinize its uses, it is inscribed in our personal experience and our elders'. But what can be said about the memories of people who inhabited the Andes more than two centuries ago? The skimpiness of the testimony we have to make do with is doubtless a great obstacle. But until recently there were other, even more basic obstacles. Understanding the uses of the past logically requires knowing that past. Earlier historiography, however, was in large part a history without a history, or, rather, a history without histories; it was predominantly macroregional in focus and statistical and taxonomic in orientation. In order to understand which memories those people used in building their hopes and longings, it was necessary to decenter our gaze in both time and space; to go back to the years before the great rebellion and recover the local histories. For it was those discrete historical experiences that insurgent Indians conjured up to do what they did and to make sense of what others did.[8] The Aymara com-

8. On the role of memory in eighteenth-century rebellions, see Stern 1987.

munities of La Paz, the indigenous peoples of the Cusco region, the peasants who inhabited the valleys and highlands of Charcas and Potosí, the dwellers of the mining town of Oruro—all of them took very different paths to get to 1780. And 1780 represented very different things for each of them. The studies that have appeared over the past fifteen years, together with the cumulative impact of several decades of research, have at last given us some insight into these worlds.[9]

This research agenda did not emerge in a vacuum, nor was it the outcome of the natural evolution of knowledge. Like earlier historiographical trends, it mirrored broader shifts in the climate of ideas and in the field of history itself. It has already been pointed out that the Shining Path experience in Peru had predisposed scholars against any brand of ethnic or cultural essentialism. By the same token, the political crisis of communism and, to a lesser extent, analytical Marxism, which the collapse of the Soviet Union and Eastern Europe very much hastened, ended up discrediting every form of economicism. Moreover, in the early 1990s the historical literature began to turn its attention to new subjects and methodologies. Such was the case of political history. Around that time numerous studies came up on the political practices of precapitalist lower-class groups and contemporary peasant societies in the underdeveloped world, a perspective that drew upon influential works by E. P. Thompson, Charles Tilly, and James C. Scott on the "moral economy," the legal and extralegal repertoires of collective action, and everyday forms of resistance to authority (Thompson 1975; Thompson 1991; Tilly 1978; Tilly 1986; Scott 1985; and Scott 1990). The research of Ranajit Guha, Sahid Amin, and other members of the Indian school of subaltern studies also demonstrated the interpretive and heuristic possibilities of semiotic analyses of popular protests as well as the counterinsurgency narratives designed to fit those events into large patterns of meaning (Guha 1983; Guha and Spivak 1988; Amin 1995).[10]

---

9. Recent works on various aspects of the pan-Andean rebellion include monographs by Andrade Padilla (1994); Cajías de la Vega (2004); Cornblit (1995); Garrett (2005); O'Phelan Godoy (1995); Robins (2002); Serulnikov (2003); Stavig (1999); Thomson (2002); and Walker (1999) and edited volumes by Fisher, Kuethe, and McFarlane (1990); Stern (1987); and Walker (1996). See also Adrián 1993; Arze 1991; Glave 1990; Glave 1999; and Penry 2006.

10. On the reception of these studies in Latin America, see Mallon 1994; Rivera Cusicanqui and Barragán 1997; and Sandoval 2009.

On the other hand, the evolution and functioning of political systems began to be linked to broad processes of social and cultural change. Around the bicentennial of the French Revolution, there was a profusion of historical writing on the progressive crisis of the political culture of the *ancien régime*, the emergence of novel bourgeois and plebeian public spheres, and the ritual and festive aspects of republicanism, all of which helped to restore to political history the prestige that it had long lost at the hands of quantitative and structural history (Hunt 1984; Baker 1990; Ozouf 1991; Chartier 1991; Farge 1992). Given that political history of any breed tends to focus on events, and the study of events lends itself to some form of narrative, one consequence of this trend was a growing preference for narrative modes of historical writing. British historian Lawrence Stone had made a compelling argument for this realignment in an early article published in 1979, "The Revival of Narrative: Reflections on a New Old History" (Stone 1979). Latin American historians interested in pursuing this path had an illustrious tradition of their own to draw upon, including, for instance, *The Black Jacobins: Toussaint L'Ouverture and the San Domingo Revolution*, by C. L. R. James; *Zapata and the Mexican Revolution*, by John Womack; and *Politics, Economics and Society in Argentina in the Revolutionary Period*, by Tulio Halperín Donghi (James 1963; Womack 1969; Halperín Donghi 1975).

Another current in Andean historiography, the shift from macroregional to local inquiries, was stimulated by the boom in microhistory that followed the publication of *The Cheese and the Worms: The Cosmos of a Sixteenth Century Miller*, by Carlo Ginzburg, and *Inheriting Power*, by Giovanni Levi. Microhistorical studies stress a reduced scale of observation, social agency over structural determinants, qualitative over quantitative analysis, and a semiotic rather than materialist conception of culture, which, to borrow from anthropologist Clifford Geertz, called for "not an experimental science in search of law but an interpretative one in search of meaning" (Ginzburg 1992; Levi 1988; Geertz 1973: 5). In the case of the Andes, this methodological shift could be anchored in rather solid foundations thanks to a wealth of ethnohistorical works, such as those by Thierry Saignes, Silvia Rivera Cusicanqui, Karen Spalding, Tristan Platt, and Luís Miguel Glave, that differed from earlier studies on Andean economic and mental structures due to their scale, use of archives, and sensitivity to historical contextualization (Saignes 1987; Saignes 1995;

Platt 1982; Spalding 1984; Rivera Cusicanqui 1992; Glave 1989).[11] Finally, postcolonial theories stemming from either history, philosophy, literary criticism, or cultural studies pushed historians to look beyond the political, institutional, and socioeconomic aspects of domination and resistance. Postcolonialists called for locating these phenomena in the wider context of the representations of otherness and the production of knowledge consubstantial with the European colonial project. Drawing on these theoretical approaches, historians began to pay particular attention to the ways in which native peoples appropriated the meaning of existing political, economic, cultural, and religious institutions, thus rebuffing binary and reified portrayals of the process by which social identities in colonial settings are fashioned.[12]

Taken together, the unequal and combined influence of political history, subaltern studies, microhistory, and postcolonial theories encouraged a remarkable flourishing of research on the role of the popular sectors in the fall of the Spanish colonial order and the formation of the new national states.[13] In the United States and British academic milieus, and much less so in the Latin American one, this paradigm shift gave rise to vitriolic debates on the benefits and limitations of what was dubbed, somewhat generically, "new cultural history" (see Deans-Smith and Joseph 1999; Knight 2002; and Joseph 2001).

The abundant scholarship on eighteenth-century Andean insurgency that has come out over the past two decades undoubtedly partakes of these vast historiographical trends. Since the following pages rest on this research, readers can assess for themselves the overall interpretation that springs from current readings of this historical event. I just wanted to offer here, before getting into the complexity of the events, a brief account of the Tupamarista revolution. For that revolution—not the events, but their meaning—have no existence outside of our questions, our interests, our prejudices. Both ours, and those of the people who came before us.

11. See also Rasnake 1988 and Abercrombie 1998.

12. Studies in this vein include Clendinnen 1987; Todorov 1992; Greenblatt 1993; Gruzinski 1993; and Mignolo 1997.

13. There is an extensive bibliography. Examples (excluding works of synthesis, collections of essays, and the studies of Andean rebellions cited above) include Mallon 1995; Guardino 1996 and 2005; Thurner 1997; de la Fuente 2000; da Costa 1994; Barragán 1999; Van Young 2001; Méndez 2005; Lasso 2007; and Di Meglio 2007.

3

....

Indian Communities Do Politics

If the Tupamarista revolution had a precise beginning, it took place not in Cusco but in a small rural village in northern Potosí.[1] Each year, in late August, the Indian population of Chayanta province would gather in a highland town named San Juan de Pocoata in order to fulfill their monetary and labor obligations toward the colonial state: the tribute and the mining mita. This province was located near the mining center of Potosí and the city of Chuquisaca, seat of the Audiencia of Charcas, the highest colonial court in the Andes. It comprised a large territory that encompasses four departments, or provinces, of present-day Bolivia, a vast region known today as Northern Potosí. Overwhelmingly populated by indigenous people, Chayanta hosted thirteen native communities, some thirty thousand souls all told. San Juan de Pocoata was one of the numerous villages the Spanish had founded across the Andes in the sixteenth century in an effort to get the Indians to abandon their old scattered settlements and live in rural towns, the way peasants did in Castile and

1. The historical information and analysis in this section draw on Serulnikov 2003: 122–156.

other parts of Europe. It was hoped that over time, under the watchful gaze of colonial officials, parish priests, and their own caciques, they would gradually be civilized. In the meantime, this massive resettlement of the native peoples would simplify the appropriation of the economic resources needed to turn the wheels of colonial society and feed the insatiable expansionist ambitions of their distant monarchs.

Like so many of the conquistadors' early schemes, this utopian project of transplanting Old World forms of social organization in the Americas—the "dream of an order" that Uruguayan intellectual Ángel Rama spoke of—ended in failure (Rama 1996: 1). It isn't that the Andean communities refused to convert to Catholicism, recognize the authority of their colonial rulers, or fulfill their economic obligations to the Crown. It's just that they did it on their own terms. Among other things, they stubbornly refused to give up their ancestral residence patterns, continuing to live in small hamlets and scattered family units alongside their agricultural lands. Moreover, the peasant society in Northern Potosí was organized in segments, extending from minor ayllus (extended kin groups) and moieties to larger ethnic units. This segmental organization was cemented by complex webs of collective landholding, reciprocity, communal labor, and ritual. As in many other Andean areas, the Indians followed a land tenure system in which each ethnic group had direct access to fields in different altitudes of the Andean landscape. Most members of the ayllus lived in the harsh highlands, at more than 3,500 meters above sea level, where they grew potatoes and other tubers and herded their llamas and alpacas. Others resided in the fertile valleys down below, where they grew maize, wheat, barley, and garden vegetables. Families would migrate from one zone to the other, following the rhythm of the planting and harvesting seasons. It was a very different conception of space from that of traditional European peasant villages, suited to the peculiarities of a topography where completely distinct ecological zones are found a few leagues apart. This economic model of ecological complementarity had for centuries provided Andean groups with a large measure of self-sufficiency. Anthropologists and historians have defined this pattern of settlement as "a vertical archipelago system" (Murra 1975: 59–115). Colonial bureaucrats used a more colloquial term: "double residence."

Most of the rural villages (or pueblos de reducción, as they were called) thus ended up becoming the hometowns for rural priests, assistants to *corregidores* (Spanish provincial governors), tax collectors, petty merchants, scribes, and a few other mestizo dwellers. Their sleepy existence was periodically disturbed when hundreds of Indians descended from their hamlets to celebrate the feasts of their patron saints, pay off their debts to the state, baptize their children, and—one might easily imagine —talk with each other about the affairs of the day. Such was the case of San Juan de Pocoata in late August. Every year, since time immemorial, peasant families from all over Chayanta had congregated in the town around the feast day of Saint Bartholomew, August 24, in order to present the corregidor with the mita workers, who, along with their wives and children, would head off that year to toil in the galleries of the Potosí mines.

In 1780, nothing went according to custom. On August 26, a violent battle broke out between the Indian communities that had gathered on the outskirts of the town and the provincial militias, a couple hundred soldiers. The Indians demanded that the corregidor, a Catalan man named Joaquín Alós, free Tomás Katari, a member of the community of Macha who was being held prisoner in the jail of the Audiencia of Charcas in the city of Chuquisaca. In the course of the skirmishes, some thirty Spaniards and mestizos lost their lives, and the rest were forced to take refuge inside the village church. Only the exhortations of the priest of Pocoata, who went out into the main plaza with an image of Christ, could somewhat soothe the crowd's spirits. During the confrontation, Alós himself was taken prisoner and led off to the village of San Pedro de Macha, a few leagues southeast of Pocoata.

Nothing that took place in Pocoata that day was spontaneous or unforeseen. Quite to the contrary, the battle had been preceded by months of open confrontation. For more than two years, the Machas, a large ethnic group of about 3,300 souls, had been demanding that their caciques be replaced by individuals who enjoyed the trust of the community. Tomás Katari was one of them. This was by no means an uncommon demand. During the eighteenth century, struggles for control of community chieftainships had resulted in countless lawsuits and local revolts throughout Upper Peru. And, as in Chayanta province, this issue would become one of the main triggers for the great rebellion of 1780, because the powers and sphere of influence of Andean caciques went far beyond the political or symbolic realms; the welfare, and even the very survival of the community depended on them. Among their many responsibilities, each year the ethnic lords elected the Indians who would work in the Potosí mines as mitayos and those who would be in charge of funding the costly religious festivities; allocated farmland to the households (the size and characteristics of the plots often determined the amount of their respective tribute quota); administered grain mills, parcels farmed collectively, and other communal economic resources; arbitrated land disputes among families and ayllus; protected the ethnic territories in the frequent conflicts with Spanish haciendas and neighboring native groups over boundary lines; and represented their communities before corregidores, tax collectors, parish priests, mine owners, and other local power groups. What happened during the eighteenth century is that all these functions increasingly fell into the hands of caciques discretionally appointed by the corregidores without consideration of their hereditary rights. (Such caciques were called interinos or intrusos.) And even those caciques who did descend from old lineages of Andean lords had no better reputations among the Indians. By the eighteenth century, hereditary caciques across the southern Andes had begun to lose the prestige they once might have held. Most of them were by then mestizos, both ethnically and culturally, due to long-standing kinship and economic ties to rural Hispanic groups, and they and their extended families tended to monopolize the best communal land. This process of social differentiation within the indigenous society prompted a growing feeling that not only particular hereditary caciques but also the hereditary principles of government themselves lacked any legitimacy.

Hence, when the Indians set out to oust their ethnic chiefs, it was not a matter of simply substituting one cacique for another; a whole world of grievances was at stake. How should agrarian resources and economic obligations be distributed among community members? What type of political criteria should dictate the access to native chieftainships? Which colonial burdens were acceptable, and which weren't? What limits should be placed on the power of Spanish officials within Indian society?

All of these matters had taken on special urgency since the middle of the century because of the conjunction of several economic trends that affected the entire Andean area. One was the steady expansion of the reparto de mercancías, or forced sale of goods, a commercial system under which provincial corregidores forcibly distributed mules, iron, clothes, coca, and other commodities to the Indians under their rule at prices far above market rates. In addition to becoming one of the harshest economic burdens—even more so than tribute, for instance—this commercial monopoly led corregidores to meddle aggressively in the appointment of caciques, for the caciques were in charge of handing out the goods to the community members and collecting the payments. It was also the beginning of a period of relative land scarcity caused by a new cycle of population growth. Mounting demographic pressures translated into a proliferation of agrarian conflicts within the indigenous communities, between neighboring communities, and between communities and haciendas. Also, as the historical literature has shown, these years saw a steady fall in the price of the agricultural commodities that Indians sold in urban markets; they had to set aside more and more of their annual harvest to earn the money needed for meeting their dues to the Crown (tribute), the Spanish governors (the reparto), and the Church (the feasts for the patron saints and other Catholic celebrations, the customary offerings to the parish, and the sacraments administered by the priests). Moreover, under the reign of Charles III, the Bourbon imperial administration undertook enormous efforts to increase colonial revenues, leading to steep hikes in the *alcabala* (a tax on the sale of goods), from 2 percent to 4 percent in 1772 and to 6 percent in 1776, and the establishment of customs houses at the entrances to cities to guarantee that the tax would be collected. Last, the rebel area mostly matched the area subjected to Potosí's mining mita. Around the time of the insurrection, silver mining was undergoing a protracted phase of production growth. Yet this growth stemmed not from the discovery of new veins of ore, or from technological innovations, but from the introduction of more brutal and sophisticated forms of forced labor.

In short, Andean communities were finding it harder and harder to bear the burdens that were raining down upon them. As their living conditions deteriorated, the corregidores, the parish priests, and especially the caciques (whether hereditary or imposed by the Spanish officials) turned into regular targets of discontent and collective violence. To make matters worse, class struggles were compounded by intense confrontations for the appropriation of peasant resources among colonial elites. The Crown, in its zeal to boost revenues from its overseas possessions, endeavored to curb both the accustomed embezzlement of tribute money by corregidores and ethnic chiefs and the economic exactions of the provincial governors and the Church (the expulsion of the Jesuits in 1767 was part and parcel of this policy). Facing mounting pressures from above, the corregidores, the rural clergy, treasury officials, and high colonial magistrates did not hesitate to fan any indigenous complaints—against the forced sale of goods, ecclesiastical fees, tribute collection, the mining mita—that might restrict their adversaries' access to peasant surpluses. The combination of inter- and intraclass battles for Indian labor and agrarian production led to a wave of social unrest that grew larger as the years of the pan-Andean rebellion approached. According to a rather outdated and partial statistic, local revolts across Peru increased from about ten in the 1750s to twenty in the next decade, then jumped to nearly seventy outbreaks between 1770 and 1779 (O'Phelan Godoy 1985).

But it is the nature of these conflicts, not their number, that tells us the most about the political culture of the colonial Andes. For popular uprisings were far from being isolated or spontaneous outbursts of violence; they were part and parcel of large patterns of political action. To begin with, native communities conceived their demands in terms of general rights, since their grievances usually stemmed not from particularly abusive individuals, but from state policies and broad socioeconomic trends. They were inclined to think that their causes of distress were shared by everyone of their same social condition—and more often than not, they were right. Second, even the most confined protest could ignite a process of politicization because virtually every social conflict in eighteenth-century Andes pushed the Indians to deal with various government agencies (corregidores, Audiencias, treasury officials, the Church, the viceroys), to experience the gap between norms and power, to test the balance of forces between them and their local rulers. To put it another way: no peasant riots failed to be preceded by protracted legal appeals, and seldom did any collective process of legal appeal fail to result in some form of collective violence. Finally, migratory movements between valleys and highlands, coresidence in Potosí while serving mita turns, community gatherings in rural villages to celebrate Catholic feasts, participation in urban markets and regional trade routes, and collective journeys to the cities to pursue lawsuits against local power groups all nurtured lively channels of communication among native peoples. Social interaction, in turn, helped spread information, complaints, and ultimately political unrest from one place to another. Hence the Andean colonial system itself prevented the creation of a localocentric worldview among the Indians that has been defined for the peasantry in general as the "parish pump," or, in reference to colonial Mexico, as *campanillismo*: "the tendency of villagers to see the social and political horizon as extending metaphorically only as far as the view from their church bell tower." (Hobsbawm 1973: 8; Van Young 2001: 483). To change their small world, Andean peoples needed to engage the world at large. What happened in 1780 is that they thought it was the world at large that needed to be changed.

In the years leading up to the battle in the town of Pocoata, almost all of the indigenous communities in Chayanta province had witnessed intense and prolonged episodes of social protest involving both court claims and popular upheaval. In 1772, for instance, a long cycle of Indian mobilization began when the colonial administration issued a new schedule of ecclesiastical fees (*arancel*) that fixed the exact amount of money and produce the clergy could charge their indigenous parishioners for religious feasts, masses, and sacraments. This move represented a concerted effort to standardize and curtail the revenues of the rural parishes. The clergy refused to implement the new tariff list, and for years thereafter many communities across the province flooded Spanish courts with complaints against material demands and abuses of power by the Church. In many instances, the Andean peoples harassed their priests to force them to abide by the new rules. Though the end result of this confrontation varied from town to town, all of the native communities got the steady backing of the Audiencia of Charcas, and with it the notion that customary Church exactions were not only unjust but also illegal. Likewise, a wave of mass protests broke out in 1774 when the provincial corregidor decided to replace the ethnic chiefs of Pocoata with the lord of the neighboring community of Moscari, a wealthy and influential cacique named Florencio Lupa. By then Lupa had amassed a considerable fortune and interacted with local ruling groups, Spanish landowners, and miners on an almost equal footing. For more than three years, the Pocoata Indians forcefully resisted the encroachment on their right to self-government. Eventually they would obtain the full support of colonial courts as they proved the misappropriation of royal tribute by both the corregidor and the cacique. They did so by resorting to a compelling resource: handing the tribute money over directly to treasury officials in Potosí. In 1777, after fierce clashes in the rural villages and countless journeys to Chuquisaca and Potosí courts, the corregidor was finally forced to remove Lupa from the Pocoata chieftainship.

The battle of Pocoata in August 1780 was far from exceptional, then, either in the general context of the Andes or in Chayanta province itself. What set the collective protest led by Tomás Katari apart was the political dynamics the conflict ultimately took on. Around the time that the Machas began to demand the removal of their ethnic lords, a Catalan man named Joaquín Alós had assumed his duties as the new corregidor of Chayanta. After an inspection tour of the province in preparation for taking office, he had warned the highest royal magistrate in Peru, Inspector General (Visitador General) Antonio de Areche, one of the architects of the Bourbon imperial policies, that he would not under any circumstances allow his authority to be undermined by the sort of protests and lawsuits that his predecessors had put up with. There were plenty of reasons for Alós to do this: like other corregidores, he had bought his office in Madrid (since the seventeenth century, the Crown had been selling the major colonial offices), and constant social upheaval would endanger the profits he hoped to make from his investment, especially the revenues from the forced sale of goods. Alós lamented in particular that Audiencia ministers and royal treasury officials, instead of punishing the rebel Pocoatas, had awarded their leaders by appointing them caciques. The reason, he said, was "the indifference with which these affairs are regarded, thwarting with any pretext, with orders and commissioned judges, the corregidores' authority" (Serulnikov 2003: 115). Hence, in early 1778, in his first public act as corregidor, when the Machas showed him some rulings they had won in Potosí and Charcas courts in favor of their claims against their caciques (no different from those obtained earlier by their Pocoata neighbors), Alós arrested them, confiscated the deeds, and had Tomás Katari whipped in the plaza of the town of Macha by the very same cacique—a mestizo named Blas Bernal— whom the higher courts had ordered the corregidor to remove from office. Then "he expressed to the concourse of all the Indians that he was their absolute Corregidor and Inspector, and that there were no Audiencia or Royal Officials; if they went to complain once more, he would hang them from his horse's stirrup" (Serulnikov 2003: 118). But to no avail. Over the ensuing months, the Machas continue to push their claims against the caciques and the corregidor in the regional courts, even at the cost of recurrent arrests and punishments. When it became apparent that these efforts were doomed to fail, they made an unprecedented decision: try their luck in a new, still untested, and far distant court, the Viceroyalty of Río de la Plata in Buenos Aires.

The long and difficult journey to that distant city to represent the Machas was undertaken by Tomás Katari. In short order Katari, who spoke no Spanish, did not belong to a noble lineage, and paid tribute like any other Indian commoner, would become the most recognizable insurgent leader in the region. When he reached Buenos Aires in the summer of 1779, accompanied by another Indian from Macha, the bureaucrats of the new Viceroyalty could not hide their perplexity. He was the first Aymara who had made it to Buenos Aires of his own accord, and they were amazed by his appearance, his attire, and above all the fact that he had walked the 1,180 miles between the highland town of Macha and the Río de la Plata basin to resolve a purely local dispute. They soon discovered, nonetheless, that what Tomás Katari had to say was of great interest to them. In two separate depositions, he described at length the caciques' tyranny, the corregidores venality, and the utter inability of the incompetent ministers of the Audiencia of Charcas and the royal treasury in Potosí to do anything about it. Viceroy Juan José de Vértiz and his legal advisers represented a new generation of enlightened administrators, determined to enforce a more rational and efficient model of colonial government. They were the bearers of modern, absolutist ideas about royal power. They believed it was imperative to put an end, once and for all, to the corruption of local officials who for centuries had regarded public service as their own personal property and their personal source of income. They may have been blind to the complexities of power relations in Andean society, but they had a grand vision of the empire as a whole, and what Katari had come to tell them was something they were ready to hear. This was particularly true regarding the intimate link between the forced sale of goods, the misappropriation of tribute revenues, and pervading social upheaval. It came only to reaffirm deep-seated beliefs in the ominous consequences of this centuries-old trade system on both the livelihood of the indigenous communities and the welfare of the royal treasury.

The viceroy therefore sent Katari back to his town with an order for the Audiencia of Charcas to designate a commissioned judge to investigate the complaints; and if the complaints proved to be true (Katari had been unable to produce any deeds from earlier appeals because corregidor Alós has confiscated them all), the caciques were to be removed immediately, Katari was to be named in their place, and eventually the corregidor himself was to be dismissed. In the meantime, Katari was to be put in charge of collecting the tribute from Macha, and, very importantly, the Audiencia was to inform Alós of "the prohibition that is forthwith imposed on him of trying, conducting, or executing any lawsuit or sentence against the commissioner, the petitioner [Tomás Katari], or anyone else who has interest, standing, or cognizance in this case" (Lewin 1957: 350).

Whereas the Machas told the enlightened magistrates of Buenos Aires the sort of story they were prepared to hear, the news they brought back with them was exactly what the colonial officials in Charcas were not about to tolerate. The creation of the Viceroyalty of Río de la Plata three years earlier, in 1776, had removed the Charcas court from the orbit of the viceroy in Lima, and hence from the splendid isolation it had enjoyed for centuries. Accustomed to reigning supreme over Andean affairs, the Audiencia ministers now saw a threat looming over their power, their preeminence, and their business opportunities with corregidores, merchants, mine owners, and hacienda owners who needed their legal support and influence. They could occasionally uphold the Indians in their conflicts with the rural elites, as they had often done in the past; but how could they allow a court with no history and no reputation, located in the remotest corner of the Spanish empire, to start meddling in the affairs of the government of Upper Peru? In 1779, when Tomás Katari returned from Buenos Aires, the Audiencia pointedly disregarded Viceroy Vértiz's orders, advising the Indian leader and the large number of Machas who had joined him in Chuquisaca to go back to Chayanta province, "in the confidence that corregidor [Alós] would attend their demands without occasioning them any harm" (Serulnikov 2003: 130).

The political culture of Spanish colonial society revolved around a fundamental dichotomy. For both ideological and material reasons, the

Crown had a vested interest in protecting the native peoples from abuses by the Hispanic ruling and economic elites as well as their own ethnic chiefs. Hence a large network of state courts and officially designated "protectors of the natives" (*protectores de naturales*) was very early on established across the core areas of the empire. In addition, over the course of the centuries there emerged a variegated group of cultural middlemen (clerks, notaries, lawyers) who earned their living by representing Indians before the tribunals and translating their complaints into Spanish legal language. But at the same time, since no independent police force existed, no legal ruling by any higher court could be enforced without vigorous displays of collective force. As the plaintiffs themselves were the ones who had to hand rural colonial officials the judicial sentences, which were usually directed against the local power brokers—more often than not against those rural officials themselves—it was unlikely that local authorities would abide by the sentences unless they felt compelled to do so. In short, the politics of violence and the politics of rights were part and parcel of the same political practice. Resorting to Spanish justice did not prevent popular revolts: rather, it granted them legitimacy.

As might be expected, when Katari and his peers returned to the province, they were not "administered justice" without themselves suffering "any harm," as the Audiencia magistrates had cynically promised them: on the contrary, the indigenous leader was arrested by corregidor Alós as soon as he set foot in Chayanta. In fact, counting on the unabashed support of regional officials, Alós had Katari arrested once again when, after freeing him, the Machas returned to both Potosí and Chuquisaca to denounce the corregidor's scandalous behavior. The Indians, to be sure, did not appeal to the colonial courts out of naïveté or a sense of weakness. They knew perfectly well what they were exposing themselves to; they chose this course because it expressed entrenched notions of justice. So it was that in June 1780, when Katari and a large group of Machas were once more heading toward Chuquisaca, the priest of Macha warned them that they were sure to be arrested as soon as they reached the city. Even though he had just spent eight months in prison in Potosí, Katari replied that "of course they should catch him, for, as he was innocent, he wished to declare his truth and his justice, for which reason he would not leave the door of the Audiencia but would stay there day after day, in the view and presence of all" (Serulnikov 2003: 123).

Indeed, on June 10, 1780, when the Audiencia judges decided to arrest him once more, all they had to do was send a constable to the main door of the courthouse to lead him to a cell inside the building.

Does this mean that the Indians had renounced the use of force? Quite the contrary. While Katari was proclaiming "his truth and his justice" alongside dozens of Machas who traveled incessantly between Chayanta and Chuquisaca to demand his release, the province grew ungovernable. The Machas went after everyone (indigenous or not) who had been complicit in their leader's travails, and they hounded all their ethnic authorities to the point of forcing them to beg the corregidor to accept their resignations. Blas Bernal, the group's main cacique, met a worse fate: he was captured and executed. The ayllu members gave their tribute money to new ethnic rulers whom they elected themselves—the same people who were heading the protest movement. The Indians re-portedly checked all the mail and guarded the entrances to the province: people could not pass through without telling them their names, their place of origin, the papers they were carrying, and the business they were on, and then their clothing and luggage were inspected. The corregidor himself was ambushed and attacked several times in June and July by thousands of Indians while traveling around the province in a futile attempt to keep order and collect tribute and debts from the forced sale of goods. During one of these assaults, he was forced to promise that Katari would be set free by the time of the annual gathering in Pocoata and that the number of goods from the reparto system would be re-duced. It is clear that by this time Katari's reputation had begun to spread far beyond the boundaries of his community. He had traveled all the way to Buenos Aires, seen the viceroy—the king's alter ego—and gained his support. He showed an unyielding resilience in the face of punishments and imprisonments. Whether supernatural, messianic fea-tures began to be attributed to him, as some historians have argued, is not known for sure. What we do know is that in less than three years his actions had turned him from an Indian commoner, known only within his community, to a symbol of the struggle against the colonial powers. That much is evidenced by the thousands of Indians from several ethnic groups of Chayanta who gathered in San Juan de Pocoata in August 1780 to demand that the corregidor keep his pledge to set Katari free.

Believing that he could dissuade the Indians through the use of force,

Alós organized a large militia company composed of mestizo and Spanish dwellers of several provincial towns. It was this company that was wiped out by the indigenous crowd when the corregidor failed to keep his word and hand Katari over on August 26. Not for nothing had they been warning him for weeks that if Katari were not freed "they would not cease to continue the disturbances they had begun, and they didn't care one bit if they died in the effort" (Serulnikov 2003: 143). Alós was caught, taken prisoner, and brought to a hill on the outskirts of the village of Macha. As a sign of public humiliation and an inversion of social hierarchies, he was forced to walk barefooted and chew coca on the way. This is what he was reduced to, the proud Spanish official who three years earlier had warned the kingdom's inspector general, the Audiencia ministers, and anyone else who would listen that he would never allow anyone to constrain his authority over the Indians. In captivity, he was forced to decree a general lowering of the forced sale of goods. He attained his freedom only after the Audiencia freed Katari and promised the Andean communities that Alós would never again return to Chayanta.

4

....

Rituals of Justice, Acts of Subversion

The ideological core of the rebellion, the underlying meaning of this collective violence, can be appreciated in two incidents that took place during the days of the uprising in Pocoata.[1] The first happened when the list of mita laborers who would be sent to Potosí that year was being drawn up. The corregidor had been insisting all along that the true goal of the rebels was to free themselves from tribute payments, mining labor, and their other obligations to the Crown; after Katari's trip to Buenos Aires, the Audiencia began to echo this view. If Indians ultimately wanted "to cast off the yoke of royal subjection," as the corregidor put it, violence was likely to erupt by the day the mining mita was scheduled to be delivered. Thus, on Saturday, August 25, Alós arranged for some two hundred soldiers to take up strategic positions while he, escorted by twelve armed men, went to perform the traditional ceremony of reviewing the mita team.

About two thousand Indians were gathered in the outskirts of Pocoata when the corregidor and his small party arrived. Yet despite his repeated

1. Historical information and analysis in this section draw on Serulnikov 2003: 148–156.

warnings, the dispatch of the mita did not provoke a single act of defiance. In the context of a long-expected clash, the uneventful dispatch of the mita to Potosí could not have been a spontaneous behavior; rather, it must have been a calculated performance, carrying a definite political message. By deferring the confrontation for a few hours, the Andean communities seemed to be showing that it was not their compliance with state economic duties that was at stake in the conflict. The sole incident that took place during the ceremony reinforced this point. When, for unclear reasons, Alós attempted to seize a mine laborer, the Indians immediately rose in his defense and rescued him. Amid threats and expressions of mockery, the communities warned the corregidor that the Indian "was a *cédula* [mita worker] and therefore could not be arrested." After centuries of Spanish rule, Andean peasants were surely aware that corregidores had no legal jurisdiction over mita laborers. But in such extraordinary political circumstances, the act bore a deeper ideological significance: the mining mita, far from being a target of mass violence, was seen as establishing a close tie between the native peoples and the king and thus as empowering the communities to dismiss the authority of abusive local officials. In this view, what rendered the corregidor (and other Spanish officials) illegitimate was not that he embodied colonial rule, as Alós had repeatedly argued, but rather the fact that he no longer did.

The second episode occurred on September 1, 1780, when Katari arrived in Macha with his official appointment as cacique that the Audiencia had granted him in exchange for the release of the corregidor. As soon as the indigenous leader reached the town, he had the decree appointing him cacique read aloud. He asked the hundreds of Indians who had gathered in Macha to obey the decisions of the Audiencia. Then he went to the parish priest's house where the corregidor was being held and, according to Alós's own account, "accompanied by innumerable Indians from all *parcialidades* [ethnic groups], even from other provinces, Katari and the others made the ceremony of asking for my pardon." Let's not be misled by the literal meaning of the word: for the Indians, "pardon" connoted not an admission of guilt but, on the contrary, a recognition of the legitimacy of his actions. Thus, after prostrating himself "at your feet with the profound submission that I should render to Royal Justice," Katari demanded that the corregidor be made to listen, in front of the whole crowd of Indians, to a reading of the decree that required him to leave Chayanta and appear before the Audiencia of Charcas. Before Katari returned to Macha, the tribunal had told him that the corregidor and his lieutenant "would never return to the province and that they would be given a [corregidor] who would look upon them with love and charity." In the past, Alós had routinely disobeyed and confiscated the rulings of higher tribunals. Now he was forced to declare aloud, in the presence of everyone, that he would obey the decree removing him from office. Then he returned the document to Katari, who kept it "for its protection" (Serulnikov 2003: 151).

Unlike other social regimes, such as slavery or medieval European serfdom, Spanish domination over the Andean peoples was expressed in elaborate public rituals by means of which the Indians manifested their submission to the Crown. This was true of the ceremonies that accompanied tribute payment, mita service, religious feasts, and the administration of the king's justice. What the encounter between Alós and Katari suggests is that the insurgency in northern Potosí was expressed through the imitation, rather than the dismissal, of those rituals. But mimicry of Western ceremonies of justice was neither a mask for an underground anticolonial conspiracy nor a mere expression of acquiescence to the ruling order. The sequence of events represented a judicial act *and* an act of political subversion. On the one hand, it featured a series of legal procedures through which genuine official decrees were obeyed and put into effect. On the other hand, the extraordinary circumstances that preceded and framed this legal ceremony completely stripped it of its function as a ritual of state authority and made it instead a mimetic act, something at once equal to and different from the reality it copies. Thus, within the framework of colonial political theater, the Andean communities met their obligations toward the monarch and abided by court orders. The performance did symbolize their submission to their European rulers, but it also indicated something that went against the very essence of colonial domination: the implementation of indigenous concepts of justice and political legitimacy, as well as the supremacy of the native peoples' power of coercion.

The profound process of political radicalization behind these events was summed up in a letter that the Indians obliged corregidor Alós to write to the Audiencia from Macha on September 3, a few hours before he was freed. In this letter, speaking through the corregidor, the Andean communities reaffirmed their promise to meet their economic obligations to the Crown and asked the Audiencia ministers to attend to Katari's requests because he was "the voice that these natives listen to" and was entirely worthy of their "protection" (Serulnikov 2006: 297). The letter also stated that a new impartial provincial governor had to be appointed and that the reduction in the forced sale of goods announced, under coercion, by Alós had to be ratified by the high colonial authorities. While these claims themselves might not have been new, the position from which they were formulated was. The corregidor remarked in his letter,

> I have endeavored to eradicate the idea they had formed, which was that Your Highness wished to send a large number of soldiers, in which case these wretches protest that *the entire Kingdom will be shaken*, for their numbers greatly surpass the number of Spaniards, all of which will be avoided if only they are not disturbed. (Serulnikov 2003: 152)

Over the coming months, the kingdom would be shaken indeed, and shaken in ways that neither the Indians nor their Spanish rulers could have foreseen at the time. But we must leave that for later. For by the time it happened, the colonial authorities in the Andes, Buenos Aires, and Lima would have even graver matters to worry about. Another focal point of rebellion—independent of the one in the Charcas region, more organized and ambitious, very different in composition and in ideology—would by then be reaching the boiling point. Its epicenter was in Cusco, the ancient capital of Incas—the civilization that, just before the arrival of the Spanish, had managed to conquer the whole territory of the Andes, and the first empire that managed to conquer the whole territory of the Andes, just before the arrival of the Spanish. The leader of this movement, Túpac Amaru, would proclaim himself a new Inca king.

5

....

The Idea of the Inca

On November 4, 1780, a bit more than two months after the battle of Pocoata, corregidor Antonio de Arriaga was presiding over the celebration of the feast of St. Charles in honor of king Charles III in a town near Tinta, the capital of the province of Canas y Canchis on Cusco's southern boundary.[1] One of the local notables attending a luncheon party at the parish priest's house was José Gabriel Condorcanqui, a cacique of the communities of Pampamarca, Surimana, and Tungasuca. José Gabriel belonged to one of several families in the region that traced their descent from ancient noble Inca lineages. He was called Túpac Amaru— so his name appears on his baptismal certificate—because he was one of the paternal-line descendants of Túpac Amaru I, the last Inca king, overthrown by the Spaniards in 1572. As a young man he had studied in the Jesuit Colegio de San Francisco in Cusco, an institution created to educate the sons of the Inca nobility. He was therefore bilingual, speaking both Spanish and Quechua, and he had received a lettered education that

1. Historical information and analysis in this section draw on Flores Galindo 2010 [1987]; O'Phelan Godoy 1985; Walker 1999; Garrett 2003; Stavig 1999; Cahill 1990 and 1996 (see references); Campbell 1987; Fisher 1966; Lewin 1957; and Serulnikov 2003.

included a smattering of Latin. In addition to his aristocratic family background and his position, José Gabriel possessed a modest fortune. He had inherited a substantial herd of mules from his father, some three hundred head, which he used to transport sugar, mercury (used in refining silver), and other merchandise over the active trade routes that linked Cusco to Potosí. He was also a landowner and had some coca fields and mining ventures, two of the most profitable activities of that era. As a cacique, he administered the economic resources of his communities and had privileged access to the indigenous labor force.

To be sure, José Gabriel was not the only one claiming kinship with the last Inca emperor. The authenticity of his title was ardently disputed by Diego Felipe Betancour, another Cusco noble who considered himself a direct descendant of the royal family. In fact, the aristocratic families from the city of Cusco and the Sacred Valley of the Incas, an important region just north of the city, thought of José Gabriel as a minor provincial cacique. For the past several years, José Gabriel had spent long periods in Lima endeavoring to establish proof of his ancestry by constructing complex family trees. In 1776 and 1777, taking advantage of his presence in the capital of the Viceroyalty, he also formally requested that the peoples under his rule be exempted from the obligation to serve in the distant Potosí mita. He argued that the extremely high economic costs of the forced migration and the terrible working conditions in the mines decimated the indigenous communities in the region. Unsurprisingly, many other caciques from Canas y Canchis province supported his petition. Though his request for relief from the mita was rejected, his suit against the Betancour family was still being aired in the colonial tribunals when the feast of St. Charles in 1780 found him sharing a table with corregidor Antonio de Arriaga.

It was said that José Gabriel did not stay to the end of the luncheon. Alleging that he had other business to attend to, he retired from the table early. In reality, he was going to join a dozen of his followers who were waiting for him at the entrance to the town. That night, on his way back to his house in Tinta, Arriaga was ambushed, taken prisoner, and carried off directly to the village of Tungasuca. There he was housed in a cell located in José Gabriel's own house (most caciques had jails built inside their residences for punishing Indians who were disobedient or had fallen into debt). The corregidor was then forced to write several letters requesting arms, munitions, and money under false pretexts. The letters also called on all the inhabitants of the region to gather in Tungasuca. His capture had been so stealthy and unexpected that his letters seem not to have awoken much suspicion. Over the following days, thousands of people of indigenous, Hispanic, and mestizo origin descended on the town. On November 9, five days after Arriaga's capture, Túpac Amaru announced publicly, in the presence of some four thousand Indians armed with slings, that the corregidor would be executed by order of the king. The king, he proclaimed, had mandated other important measures as well. In effect, a royal edict was read, in Quechua and Spanish, stating that the monarch "has ordered that Don Antonio Arriaga lose his life because of his harmful behavior" and "that there be no alcabala, customs, or the Potosí mita" (Walker 1999: 35).

The royal proclamation, it goes without saying, was a fake. No one had sent any such orders. We cannot know how many believed it to be authentic, but the fact is that, on that very day, on a gallows erected for the occasion, the corregidor was hanged in the presence of a large crowd. It is not hard to imagine that, in the eyes of the thousands of Indians who were present at the ceremony, a transformation must have begun to take shape: the man presiding over the ceremony was no longer José Gabriel Condorcanqui, just one of the many caciques in the Cusco area; he was becoming Túpac Amaru II, a descendant of the last Inca emperor, perhaps himself a new Inca.

The reader may have noticed certain parallels in the public ceremonies that set the rebellions of Charcas and Cusco in motion. Some historians have emphasized that Tomás Katari and Túpac Amaru undertook similar journeys, both physically and ideologically. For one thing, each traveled to the capital of his Viceroyalty—Buenos Aires for Katari, and Lima for Túpac Amaru—in order to plead his claims before the highest magistrates in the land. Even though Túpac Amaru's complaints against the mita failed, his actions before the viceroy of Peru must have awakened a sense of approval, perhaps of admiration, similar to those of Tomás Katari before the viceroy of Río de la Plata. In addition, both leaders referred to orders from higher authorities when they set out to deal with their respective corregidores: Katari by dismissing Joaquín Alós, and Túpac Amaru by executing Antonio de Arriaga. Lowering or abolishing the forced sale of goods, the primary source of income for provincial governors, was explicitly mentioned in both episodes. Finally, both rebellions were carried out not against the king but actually in the king's name.

Yet behind these parallels, equally significant differences emerge. As seen above, the Chayanta uprising formed part of an ongoing political process. The battle of Pocoata was the foreseeable and foreseen corollary of that process. Alós's ejection from the province was simultaneously an act of sedition and a genuine legal ceremony. The proclamations that were read and carried out there were authentic—as authentic as the ones that the corregidor himself had explicitly repudiated over the preceding months and years. A tight articulation between violence and law lay at the very heart of the insurgent movement, and the Indians took pains to make it visible at every step. On the other hand, the Cusco rebellion three months later—though it did not come out of the blue, as we will soon see—was a secret conspiracy and was carried out by surprise, independently of any concrete dispute between Arriaga and the peoples under his rule. It was done in the name of the king, but an implausible king who had little to do with the monarch's real image. How many people could have believed that Charles III would order an ordinary provincial cacique to execute his corregidor and thus to eliminate at the stroke of a pen some of the main sources of royal revenues? If the final encounter between Katari and Alós constituted the mimesis of a legal act, Arriaga's execution represented the inversion of the established order: the descendants of the ancient lords of the land, headed by the descendant of the last of their emperors, took on the power to decide who should govern the kingdom, and how. It is possible that the Indians really believed that these decisions would not upset the king (in many precapitalist and Old Regime societies the peasantry and other popular groups tended to think that their monarchs were wise and just on principle and that those who governed in their names were the ones who ruined the world behind their backs). But there should have been little doubt about the actual origin of those decisions. The peasant movement in Charcas raised the question of the legitimate forms of government; the uprising led by Túpac Amaru II, the question of sovereignty.

What accounts for these differences? The answer seems to lie in the peculiar social realities of southern Peru. In the Cusco area, two distinctive features shaped the relationship between the indigenous population and colonial society on the eve of the Tupamarista revolution. The first was what has been defined as the Inca cultural revival. Historical research has revealed that images of the Incas and Andean cultural motifs became increasingly visible in Peru over the course of the eighteenth century. This growing prominence revealed itself in both popular and elite artistic expressions, including paintings and murals, textile designs, clothing, and qeros (polychrome Andean drinking vessels, usually wooden or clay). It was also seen in the wide circulation of books such as Royal Commentaries of the Incas, a work published in 1617 that exalted the Inca civilization, written by "El Inca" Garcilaso de la Vega, the son of a Spanish conquistador and an Inca noblewoman, a niece of the emperor Huayna Capac (Vega 1966 [1609–1617]). Túpac Amaru, like many other Cusco nobles of the era, had read it. Just as important, the Andean imperial tradition was evoked in public ceremonies (dances, drama performances, religious celebrations) in which most social groups in Cusco (Indians, mestizos, creoles, Spaniards) were involved as direct participants or audience members. For example, during this period it came into vogue for Andean lords to have their portraits painted in poses that showed them decked out in clothes and emblems of power from the era of Inca rule. According to the bishop of Cusco, even the Christian deities were dressed in Inca attire during Corpus Christi and the fiesta of Santiago.[2] The colonial state contributed decisively to keeping the memory of the pre-Hispanic past vibrant and meaningful by continuing to grant privileges to the native aristocracy and by allowing the Inca tradition to be taught in schools for caciques—including the school where Túpac Amaru studied, the Colegio de San Francisco de Borja in Cusco, whose eighteenth-century murals were filled with images of the ancient Inca kings. Though little is known about how Indian commoners processed this phenomenon, it is clear that they were actively involved in the public celebrations, as were the indigenous nobility and the white elites. It has even been suggested that, for indigenous people, theater began to replace ritual as the main vehicle for communal identity (Flores Galindo

2. Santiago (St. James the Greater), the patron saint of Spain, was credited by the conquerors with personally playing a crucial role in the conquest of Cusco through his miraculous appearance in the midst of a crucial battle. Dressing his image in an Inca tunic was a striking cultural appropriation.

2010 [1987]). In short, for the people of Cusco, the sudden advent of a figure such as Túpac Amaru II may have been unexpected, but it would also have been perfectly intelligible.

The second feature peculiar to this regional society was the high social standing of the native aristocracy among both indigenous peoples and white settlers. Their joint celebration of pre-Columbian legacies actually formed part of a wider pattern of cultural and economic interaction. Like José Gabriel Condorcanqui, most Andean lords were bilingual, literate mestizos who over the centuries had built well-established social and kinship networks with the creole elites. Some caciques owned haciendas and mines and participated as partners, rather than as subordinate agents, in commercial enterprises alongside Spanish officials and businessmen. In the 1770s, after decades of petitions, several prestigious Cusco noble families, as well as the great cacique lineages of the Collao (the Lake Titicaca region some two hundred miles southwest of Cusco), managed to get some of their members accepted into the Catholic priesthood, one of the most prominent symbols of assimilation and economic success. By contrast, in the Charcas area farther south, even the most prominent caciques were seen by the Hispanic sectors as more or less rustic characters: rich and powerful, perhaps, but lacking the lineage and education to be treated as equals. In this sense, a study of marriage strategies among the Cusco native elites has concluded that "the Indian nobles were thought of as the pinnacle of indigenous society, but the legal barrier that separated them from creole Peru turned out to be more porous at the personal and family levels than the social boundary that the Indian nobles had erected between themselves and the commoner Indians" (Garrett 2003: 26). At the same time, though, Indian commoners do not seem to have questioned their traditional caciques' authority. To judge from the rarity of collective protests against them during the eighteenth century, their legitimacy was more solid here in southern Peru than it was to the south of Lake Titicaca, where the ethnic lords (whether hereditary or imposed by the corregidores) were at the very heart of political upheaval both before and during the great rebellion. As a whole, the indigenous aristocracy of Cusco in the years leading up to 1780 enjoyed a level of social prestige unmatched anywhere else in the Andes.

It could be argued that Cusco society in the years before the Túpac

Amaru rebellion was at the point of greatest balance between the Andean nobility and the creole elite in the history of Peru, in terms of their comparative social status, economic power, and cultural prestige. Peruvian historian Alberto Flores Galindo has argued that "a Cuzco noble was considered as important as a Spanish noble" (Flores Galindo 2010 [1987]: 87). Though the statement might be a bit hyperbolic, it calls our attention to a singular moment in the evolution of interracial relations in the Andean world. The phenomenon that lay at the origin of the political cataclysm of 1780, and that the cataclysm itself turned into archeological ruins, was the relatively equal standing of indigenous and Hispanic elites and the consequently equal stature of their respective cultural traditions. It is true that eighteenth-century creole nationalists, as well as postindependence caudillos such as Agustín Gamarra and Andrés de Santa Cruz, exalted the ancient pre-Columbian civilizations as a way to construct new forms of collective identity for themselves. But there is a crucial difference: prior to the Túpac Amaru uprising, the celebration of the Inca past in Cusco did not resemble an inverted image of the irredeemable cultural primitivism of contemporary Indians. Colonial Cusco society recognized a tangible continuity between past and present, a continuity expressed in both the prestige and visibility of Andean traditions and the political prominence of the Andean elites. Moreover, the Inca cultural revival was not a paternalistic discourse promoted by sectors unconnected to native society, as twentieth-century indigenismo was; it was closely associated with Indians themselves. What all this means is that a deeply rooted awareness of cultural pride and social prestige, rather than marginalization and disfranchisement, lay behind the political radicalization of large sectors of native society. People decided to rise up against the established order out of a sense of empowerment, not deprivation. To be sure, the attachment to Inca symbols and political legacies did not necessarily translate into adhesion to the pan-Andean insurrection. In fact, virtually all the caciques belonging to the most traditional and prestigious Inca lineages from the Cusco and Collao regions remained loyal to the Crown during the rebellion. The larger point here is, however, that as Andean cultural traditions acquired greater prominence and greater symbolic power, they ceased to function as marks of subalternity. Ultimately it was this gradual questioning of the notions of racial inferiority that enabled the conception and diffusion of neo-Inca aspirations.

These sociocultural processes went hand in hand with equally consequential economic and political developments. As in the rest of the Andean area, the expansion of the forced distribution of goods, falling prices for the products Indians sold in the marketplace, and growing demographic pressures all weighed heavily on the peasant economy. Not surprisingly, land disputes between native communities and haciendas and collective protests against corregidores, often stoked by parish priests, began to mount. In addition, the inclusion of the Andean peoples from southern Peru in the distant Potosí mining mita had always been a bitter pill (hence Túpac Amaru's fruitless legal efforts to obtain an exemption). The social discontent, moreover, was by no means limited to the native population. The transfer of Upper Peru to the jurisdiction of the newly created Viceroyalty of the Río de la Plata, and the consequent articulation of silver mining to the Atlantic, disrupted the customary commercial networks that for centuries had linked Lima to the southern Peruvian highlands and on to Potosí. Every social sector was affected by this reorganization. Channeling exports and imports through the port of Buenos Aires caused the major productive activities of Cusco (sugar, coca, textiles) to grow less and less competitive in the Andean markets. At the same time, since the mid-eighteenth century the local creole elites had suffered increasing marginalization from public offices in government, the military, and the clergy due to the systematic favoritism toward Peninsular Spaniards promoted by Bourbon absolutist policies. Sharp increases in the alcabala and the erection of customs houses at the entrances to the cities to guarantee its more efficient collection, as well as a hike in alcohol taxes and the creation of a state monopoly on tobacco sales, only aggravated the situation for agrarian and textile producers, craftspeople, merchants, and consumers of all ethnic and social affiliations.

The accumulation of grievances from such numerous and diverse groups gave rise to a generalized climate of discontent against the Spanish government and its direct beneficiaries (great merchants, Peninsular officials, corregidores), which in turn translated into pervading political unrest. Thus, in 1777, the indigenous communities in Urubamba province, north of Cusco, rebelled against the forced distribution of goods carried out by their corregidor. Several mestizos and creoles were also implicated in the protest. In January 1780, after a customs house was erected at the entrance of the southern Peruvian city of Arequipa, the plebeian and patrician sectors alike rose up in a violent revolt that became known as "the rebellion of the *pasquines*" (named for the pasquinades, or satirical handbills, that appeared around the city before the uprising). The rebels held control of the city for several days. A number of pasquinades also appeared in Cusco around the same time, and for the same reasons; the city was awash in rumors that there would be riots. Two month later, the Cusco authorities discovered the so-called "conspiracy of the silversmiths." Appealing to the widely held resentment against the customs house, Lima authorities, and colonial rule in general, a group of creole and mestizo artisans, shopkeepers, and hacienda owners, as well as Indians from the region, began to plot a popular uprising. The threat was serious enough that, after it was discovered, the main leaders of the conspiracy were hanged in the city of Cusco.

So in early November 1780, when Túpac Amaru called for an insurrection against the colonial administration evoking Inca political symbols, the people of Cusco had both old and new, cultural and socioeconomic, reasons to listen. This may account for the astonishing alacrity, considering all that was at stake, with which tens of thousands of people responded to his call. During the days when Arriaga was being tried and executed, a large crowd, ready to join the revolt, gathered in the town of Tungasuca. Who were they? Most of Túpac Amaru's followers were Indian commoners. The epicenter of the movement was in Canas y Canchis and Quispicanchis, which were populated by numerous native communities. It has been calculated that 85 percent of the indigenous troops came from these two provinces (Stavig 1999: 251). Although mestizos, urban Indians, and individuals from various social backgrounds joined the insurrection, its core from the start comprised members of the indigenous communities: people who lived on communal lands, paid tribute, were subject to the mita and the forced sale of commodities, and were under the rule of Andean lords. It was precisely those Andean lords who led the insurgency. As in all rebel areas, not only men were mobilized, but also their wives and children. The structure of the rebel army thus largely reproduced the Andean social structure.

On November 11, two days after the public execution of Antonio de Arriaga, the rebel forces went on the march. From Tinta they headed north to Quiquijana, capital of the neighboring province of Quispicanchis in the Vilcamayo River valley. The provincial corregidor, informed of the fate of his colleague from Canas y Canchis, managed to escape. On the way back to Tungasuca, Túpac Amaru ordered his followers to attack and destroy two *obrajes*. Obrajes were textile mills, usually attached to haciendas, that employed semislave labor: mita workers sent by Indian communities and prisoners condemned to hard labor. They functioned as productive units as well as detention centers. Some came to employ hundreds of workers. Obrajes competed against *chorrillos*, small-scale textile mills attached to community lands that were controlled by the Indians themselves. Obrajes and chorrillos fought over the chance to supply southern Andean cities with low-quality fabric, or "cloth of the land," as it was then called. Canas y Canchis and Quispicanchis hosted the largest number of obrajes and chorrillos in Peru. It comes as no surprise, then, that Túpac Amaru proclaimed, as one of the obrajes was being destroyed, "in the presence of the several caciques of the neighboring towns who by his order had gathered there, . . . that his commission intends not only to hang five corregidores but also to demolish the obrajes" (Lewin 1957: 453). After freeing the prisoners and setting fire to the buildings, he distributed the cloth among those who participated in the action.

The news that corregidor Arriaga had been executed and that the Tupamarista army was on the move spread like wildfire through the region, instilling panic in the Spanish population. On November 12, only three days after Arriaga's execution, the Cusco city council met to discuss the "horrific excess" in Tungasuca (*Colección documental del bicentenario de la revolución emancipadora de Túpac Amaru* 1980: 1:69). The council members resolved to request that regular army detachments be sent immediately from Lima and to organize a local fighting force composed of city militia companies, volunteers, and some eight hundred Indians and mestizos mobilized by loyalist caciques. Part of this force was immediately dispatched to the south in order to imprison Túpac Amaru. On November 17, it arrived in Sangarará, a small village north of Tinta. The army commanders decided to spend the night camped out next to the village church. They did not imagine that when they woke up the next day they would be surrounded by rebel forces, their strength variously estimated at between six thousand and twenty thousand Indians. What they did then was what anyone would have done under such circumstances: take refuge inside the church. In Spanish America, as in Europe at that time, temples were considered inviolable places of sanctuary. Túpac Amaru demanded their immediate surrender and insisted that everybody exit the building and come out into the plaza. The Cusco soldiers refused it. A furious battle then broke out, in the course of which the church caught fire. According to some estimates, more than five hundred soldiers died, including some twenty Spaniards. Many perished when the building roof and walls caved in; others were massacred by stone and spear as they tried to flee.

The battle of Sangarará, because of its timing (barely a week after Arriaga's execution) and its appalling level of violence, immediately became a battle over symbols. Túpac Amaru went to great lengths to show that the burning of the church had been accidental, that he had offered the Cusco soldiers a chance to surrender peacefully, and that safe conduct passes had been given to the women and children. He could argue in his defense that many of the prisoners had indeed been healed and set free just a few days after the conflagration. No matter what Túpac Amaru said, for his enemies Sangarará became the emblem of what was at stake: Indians against whites, apostates against Christians. For instance, an eyewitness said that those who escaped the "voracious flames" consuming the church "fell into the hands of the no less voracious rebels. The universal slaughter, the pitiful groans of the dying, the bloodthirstiness of the enemy, the fragments of flames—in short, everything that occurred that unfortunate day provoked horror and commiseration, sentiments never felt by the rebels; blinded by fury and thirsty for blood, they only thought of stabbing all the whites" (Walker 1999: 38). On November 17, the bishop of Cusco, Juan Manuel Moscoso, excommunicated Túpac Amaru. He declared the rebel leader "incendiary of the public chapels and of the church of Sangarará," "traitor to the King," and "usurper of the Royal Rights" (Lewin 1957: 460–461). Whosoever aided or abetted him would also be excommunicated. The edict was posted on the front doors of all the churches in the region. The bishop's reaction is particularly telling, for during the months leading up to the rebellion Moscoso and corregidor Arriaga had been involved in vitriolic disputes over economic and jurisdictional issues —a typical example of the battles over peasant resources and state-Church tensions unleashed by the expansion of the forced sale of goods system and the Crown's growing control over ecclesiastical revenues. During the early days of the uprising, Túpac

Amaru tried to capitalize on this power struggle among colonial elites by sending numerous letters to the clergy and distributing edicts declaring that he was against the corregidores, the forced sale of goods, and other colonial exactions, but not against the Church or Christian customs, "to which we are all obliged" (Lewin 1957: 466–470). Yet it took only one week for the magnitude of the indigenous movement to persuade secular and ecclesiastic authorities to set their differences aside.

After Sangarará, the rebellion spread south. Going against the opinion of his wife, Micaela Bastidas, who was one of his top lieutenants and who urged him to attack Cusco before the city could strengthen its defenses and the regular army arrived from Lima, Túpac Amaru decided to march to the Collao, the region bordering Lake Titicaca. The Tupamarista troops advanced on the provinces of Lampa, Carabaya, and Azángaro. Along the way they took possession of many towns and established direct contact with the local communities. The social structure of the Collao was more like Upper Peru than like Cusco; the Indians here did not hesitate to open up to the entering insurgents even in the face of open opposition from many of their caciques. An emblematic example was the town of Azángaro, where Túpac Amaru made a triumphal entrance on December 13. The rebel leader was especially bent on destroying the properties of Diego Choqueguanca, a powerful cacique whose extended family included hacienda owners, merchants, and even members of the clergy. Choqueguanca had opposed the rebellion from the outset. Aided by indigenous communities and facing weak resistance from provincial corregidores and local militias, the Tupamarista forces quickly seized control of nearly the entire high plateau of southern Peru. Their military campaign was indeed far from conventional. Their usual procedure was to send emissaries and proclamations to each rural town calling on its people to rebel. Only after they did this would Túpac Amaru make his triumphal entry. The battle of Sangarará—a frontal clash between royalists and Tupamaristas—was the exception, not the rule. It has been rightly observed that there was no "clear demarcation between native peoples' spontaneous uprisings and Túpac Amaru's military campaigns" (Flores Galindo 2010 [1987]: 96). Military battles were to a large extent indistinguishable from popular revolts.

The proclamations and edicts that the Tupamaristas issued to win over the people of Peru tended to revolve around some basic themes:

theirs was a war against the Europeans, against corregidores, against trade monopolies, against the new customs houses where alcabalas were being forcefully collected, and against many other colonial burdens. It was not against the creoles, the Catholic Church, or the monarch. But the Indian commoners—especially in the provinces of the Collao, where the movement was less hierarchical than in the Cusco area—tended to have a broader understanding of who their enemies were: great land-lords, obraje owners and administrators, tax collectors, caciques, and other local chiefs all became targets of popular violence. The fact that most of these targets were "Peruvians" (a recurring reference in the Tupamarista political language) didn't seem to impress the insurgents much. It was their class position, not their birthplace, that counted. Túpac Amaru, for his part, continued to insist for some time that he was just doing what the king had instructed him to do: eradicate the rampant corruption of colonial officials and, if need be, the colonial officials themselves. But it was also true that after the battle of Sangarará he had a portrait painted of himself and Micaela Bastidas with all the insignias and symbolic attributes of the Inca kings. Although this kind of painting was not that unusual among the eighteenth-century Inca nobility, in this extraordinary historical context the particular political meaning of such imagery could not have been lost on anyone. Moreover, studies of the Tupamaristas' edicts and letters have shown that, as the weeks went by, references to Charles III grew more and more infrequent. Historians disagree as to whether Túpac Amaru's true leanings were separatist or autonomist—whether he sought emancipation from the colonial me-tropolis or wanted to remain subject to the Crown under new political arrangements. But even if he imagined the new Kingdom of Peru to be part of the Spanish Crown, it was obvious that its bonds to the monarchy would be of a completely different order from the existing ones, much more loose and abstract. At the very least, that Kingdom of Peru would be governed not by a European but by an Inca. There was his portrait with Micaela Bastidas for all to see.

In Cusco, these fine ideological distinctions mattered little. Everyone understood that no matter what statements of principle Túpac Amaru made, the world would be very different if the rebellion prevailed. And the immense majority of the insurgent movement's potential allies in colonial society—the Peruvians to whom Túpac Amaru addressed his pleas—showed little or no inclination to be part of that world. Not only the upper-class creoles (hacienda owners, provincial officials, merchants, lawyers) but also large segments of urban popular groups felt that their shared outrage at the Bourbon imperial policies was not a reason to bet on the success of a revolutionary movement manned by armed indigenous peoples and led by a self-proclaimed Inca king. The battle of Sangarará and the subsequent campaign in the Collao revealed both the nature and the magnitude of the threat. So the city dwellers of Cusco joined the militias, stockpiled food and provisions, and prepared to resist.

6

....

Cusco under Siege

Túpac Amaru returned from his campaign in the provinces of the Collao in mid-December.[1] By then the situation in Cusco was starting to deteriorate. While waiting for regular troops to arrive from Lima, the Cusco authorities were rushing to form large militia detachments. Under the command of the War Council (Junta de Guerra), some three thousand men were mobilized. On December 20, thanks mainly to their highly superior firepower, these local royalist forces succeeded in defeating an insurgent unit near the town of Ocongate in Quispicanchis province. It was the first important military setback for the Tupamarista army. Aware of the increasing strength and organization of their enemy and the imminent arrival of viceregal regiments, at last Túpac Amaru set out to attack the city. On December 28, 1780, the ancient Inca capital awoke to the news that some thirty thousand Indians were encamped in the heights of Picchu on the outskirts of Cusco.[2] The last time Cusco had witnessed

1. Historical information and analysis in this section draw on Flores Galindo 2010; O'Phelan Godoy 1985; Walker 1999, 2008; Garrett 2003; Stavig 1999; Campbell 1987; Fisher 1966; Lewin 1957; and Serulnikov 2003.
2. Roughly a mile from the center of Cusco, Picchu is one of the many hills ringing the city; it is not to be confused with the archaeological site of Machu Picchu.

such a thing was in 1536, when an indigenous army led by Manco Inca, a son of the last Inca emperor, Huayna Capac, came close to expelling the conquistadors who had captured the city four years earlier. Few Cusco residents seemed to believe that they could withstand a frontal attack by such a massive force. A frontal attack was not what Túpac Amaru had in mind, however. Following the same military tactics that had proved so effective up until then, he sent several emissaries to start negotiations with the secular and religious authorities in the hope that the city would surrender, or perhaps that the plebeian groups would rise up and join the rebellion. He also issued some pronouncements urging urban dwellers to let the rebel forces enter the city without bloodshed. Insofar as these pronouncements were intended to attract the support of nonindigenous persons, one would expect the goals of the movement to be framed in the most inclusive, far-reaching manner. But this was not yet the case. It is indicative of the political outlook at the heart of the disturbances that the central arguments continued to emphasize the aspirations of the Andean peoples. Túpac Amaru did endeavor to draw the sympathy of the creole elites by promising that should the rebellion succeed, the Spanish king's sovereignty would not be brought into question. He even gave assurances that the trade relations between Cusco and the Viceroyalty of Río de la Plata would continue as usual. Nonetheless, the overriding theme of the writings was the grievances and claims of the natives. For example, on January 3, he sent a letter to the Cusco city council in which he noted, "Mine is all that remains of the blood of the Incas, kings of this kingdom," one fact that had driven him to fight so fiercely against the corregidores and their repartos. He demanded that the provinces be administered by governors "from the Indian nation itself" and that an Audiencia and a Viceroy be set up in Cusco "so that the Indians might have access to justice closer at hand." These demands were linked to a larger historical narrative, for the abuses had begun not recently but long ago. They had originated in the flagrant disregard for the laws that the Spanish kings had passed since the conquest to protect the Andean peoples: "This is so well known that it needs no further proof than the tears that these wretched people have been weeping for three centuries." To remove these ills, the discourse of the conquest had to be turned upside down: the kingdom should now be headed by the conquered, led of course by Túpac Amaru himself, "all that remains of the blood of the Incas" (the letter cited is printed in Lewin 1957: 456).

Túpac Amaru's arguments won him little support inside the city. The image of a proclaimed Inca heading an indigenous army, upholding the rights of the natives, would hardly seem compelling to most creoles and mestizos. Thus, for instance, as one of Túpac Amaru's envoys endeavored to set bishop Moscoso at ease by arguing that they had no intention of causing offense to the city or to the "patriots," the bishop replied "that this rebel [Túpac Amaru] should be told that the city had subjects very loyal to His Majesty who would punish his audacity, as he would discover in short order" (Lewin 1957: 457). Moscoso's perception of the political leanings of the city's residents was not far off. To be sure, some groups at times appeared ready, in view of the huge disparity in troop strength, to accept a negotiated surrender. Certainly, too, the Cusco elites worried about how the urban lower class would behave when the hour of truth arrived. Nevertheless, all these suspicions vanished on January 1, 1781, when the first detachment of some two hundred regular army soldiers from Lima finally arrived in Cusco. The determination to resist to the end then prevailed.

The decisive battle took place on January 8. The royalist troops attacked the Indian positions on Picchu and, after two days of intense combat, managed to put them to flight. How can the defeat of such a large and well-organized insurgent force be explained? It has been pointed out that the insurgents were unable to carry out a projected pincer maneuver against Cusco because of the defeat of two rebel columns on their way to the area. Heavy rainfall and food shortages could have also made increasingly difficult to sustain the siege. But there were less circumstantial factors at play. Analyzing the causes of the failure, one eyewitness pointed to the social composition of the urban companies. He maintained that the militias disillusioned Túpac Amaru with regard to his ability to attract followers from significant sectors of Cusco society: "He recognized that the whole city without exception of nobles or plebeians, of the great or the little, of men or women, was resolved to spill their last drop of blood for their freedom and King: he was faced with all the force that he never thought we might possess" (Lewin 1957: 459). This lack of significant support for the rebels' cause beyond the indigenous population could also be seen in the scarcity of rebel personnel trained in using firearms. The insurgents were armed with the weapons they had been able to seize from royalist forces in combat or had found in the town they had occupied. But in addition to the shortage of arms—a clear military disadvantage, no doubt—there was also the fact that few Indians knew how to handle muskets and rifles effectively; most only employed slings, clubs, and spears. In this regard, the services of the mestizos and creoles were absolutely vital. The limited firepower of the insurgent forces can be seen as a sign of the rare participation of nonindigenous groups among their ranks. In fact, the main creole contingent in the rebel army, essentially the local militia of Tinta, fled during the final battle, taking with them most of the weaponry. Back in their hometown, they announced a counterrebellion (Cahill 2003: 84). To operate the artillery, Túpac Amaru even had to make use of captured prisoners. Their complete disloyalty to his cause was reflected in acts of sabotage with fateful military consequences. The Cusco city council, for example, recognized that one of the gunners and artillery men on the enemy side had purposefully damaged the guns and misaimed the cannons "with the stratagem of not harming us" (Lewin 1957: 461). This experience may have pushed Túpac Amaru to come to terms with the ultimate realities of the conflagration underway. In sharp contrast to his previous policy, in the aftermath of the failed assault on Cusco he reportedly ordered his troops to kill all creoles without exception (Cahill 2003: 86).

It is also crucial to note that, although numerous Andean peoples of the region backed the rebellion, their support was by no means unanimous. In Canas y Canchis, Túpac Amaru's home province, the vast majority of indigenous groups and their caciques joined the uprising (although even here there were two communities, Coporaque and Sicuani, that remained royalist). In neighboring Quispicanchis, on the other hand, only about half joined. It has been calculated that in the province of Cusco, excluding the city and its immediate environs, some 28,500 Indians joined the rebellion, but 36,750 supported the royalist cause (Stavig 1999: 250–251). In some provinces north of Cusco, such as Cotabambas and Abancay, few or no communities rose up. Indians living on haciendas tended to remain neutral. As has been shown for peasant movements in other times and places, the poorest and most vulnerable were much more hesitant to rebel than those who enjoyed some measure of political autonomy and who controlled some economic resources of their own. It is possible, moreover, that the swift reaction of colonial authorities to the outbreak of mass violence helped in part to neutralize the causes of social discontent. After the disaster of Sangarará, the Cusco authorities hastened to declare the abolition of the forced distribution of goods, forgive debts stemming from this commercial system, eliminate the customs houses, and prohibit the collection of church tithes from Indians.

At the other end of the social ladder, the noble Inca families of the Sacred Valley, the most prestigious and prosperous members of the indigenous aristocracy, proved reluctant to risk it all on a revolt of commoner Indians headed by a second-rate provincial noble. More important, these royalist caciques seem to have enjoyed no less support among the members of their communities than the rebel caciques did among theirs. Two prominent examples are Pedro Apu Sahuaraura, cacique of the parish of Santiago in Cusco and descendant of the most prestigious noble Inca line, and Mateo Pumacahua, cacique of the pueblo of Chinchero in the province of Urubamba. Both led the Indians under their rule into battle against Túpac Amaru. Pedro Apu Sahuaraura lost his life defending the city; Pumacahua, as we will see in the last chapter, would play a key political role in the years to come. Likewise, the arrival of thousands of Indians from the neighboring province of Paruro in support of the royalist forces during the decisive battle for Picchu did much to seal the rebels' fate. It was said that their appearance caused many to desert the Tupamarista ranks. A Spanish chronicle noted that "this great relief, at such an opportune time, heartened our troops, and upon observing all this, the enemy diminished their arrogant audacity" (Lewin 1957: 458). Coincidentally, Túpac Amaru explained that he had been forced to retreat from Cusco for lack of personnel competent in using rifles and artillery, but also "because they put the Indians in the front lines to serve as cannon fodder" (Lewin 1957: 461).

On January 10, 1781, Túpac Amaru's dreams of a triumphal entrance into the ancient capital of the Inca empire came to an end. Inexorably, the rebellion in the Cusco area would lose steam from then on. The royalist forces, composed of a combination of detachments of the regular Spanish army, local militias, and indigenous troops led by loyalist caciques such as Mateo Pumacahua, would take the offensive. The region would remain in a state of agitation for several more months, but the failure of the siege would displace the center of the insurrection southward. Within the Viceroyalty of Peru, the provinces of the Collao region would become the main theater of conflict. Farther south, in Charcas, the first focal point of insurgency, headed by Tomás Katari, was reaching its peak just at this time for reasons largely unrelated to the events of Cusco. And very soon—first in Oruro, then in La Paz—other revolts would break out, even larger and more violent.

7

"Perverted in These Revolutions"

By the time that the Tupamarista insurgency was rattling the provinces of Cusco and the Collao, the situation to the south, in the Charcas region, was deteriorating week by week.[1] After Joaquín Alós, the corregidor of Chayanta province in northern Potosí, was expelled and Tomás Katari was installed as the new cacique of the Macha community, the social order in Chayanta collapsed. In southern Peru, the dividing line between Túpac Amaru's military campaigns and peasant revolts may have been rather fuzzy, but in Chayanta, and Charcas at large, the revolution was simply the result of the proliferation of local uprisings. Ever since September 1780, following the examples of Macha that year and Pocoata a few years earlier, virtually every community in Chayanta (Laymi, Puraca, Moscari, Chayantaca, Sicoya, Sacaca, San Pedro de Buena Vista, Moromoro, Ocurí, and Pitantora) pursued, captured, and overthrew its caciques, whether hereditary or imposed by the corregidores. Many were dragged off to Macha, the political capital of the uprising, for Katari to decide what to do with them. The egalitarian, representative

1. Historical information and analysis in this section draw on Serulnikov 2003: 157–185.

concepts of government underpinning the movement are illustrated by the argument leveled by the community of Laymi against their cacique, Marcos Soto, a descendant of an ancient family of Andean lords. They told the indigenous leader, "We no longer want as our governor someone from whom we experienced so much mistreatment and trouble, we want instead someone to be named *whom the community has chosen, who should be from our own class*" (Serulnikov 2003: 170, emphasis added). What this statement reveals is a view of ethnic authority as based on merit and conduct, not lineage and hereditary rights. The battle of Pocoata thus had not changed the insurgents' political aims so much as their political practices. Instead of traveling to Chuquisaca or Potosí to press their cases before the high colonial magistrates, they now headed to Macha to confer with Tomás Katari.

The Indians of Moscari also beat and imprisoned their cacique, Florencio Lupa. However, instead of handing him over to Katari and the parish priest of Macha as the other communities did with their caciques, after a nighttime meeting they decided on something else: "In the midst of the confusion, shouting, and uproar, they cut his head off" (Serulnikov 2003: 159). They went on to display his head on a cross in the outskirts of the city of Chuquisaca. Let us recall that Lupa was the most powerful cacique in the province—one of the few members of native society whom the Chuquisaca residents knew by name, and the only one whom the corregidores and the hacienda and mine owners of that province treated as an equal. When, on the morning of September 6, the authorities and city neighbors discovered the head of the powerful cacique, they thought it was the end of the world. Collective panic made some believe they had seen "a considerable number of Indians raising flags and blowing cornets with the obvious purpose of falling into this neighborhood and invading it. People believe that these Indians are coming from the rebellious province of Chayanta" (Serulnikov 2003: 54). No such multitude existed, nor had Katari had anything to do with the action (in fact, the people who carried it out returned directly to Moscari without stopping in Macha). But even though their fears died down as the hours went by, Lupa's execution made the Audiencia magistrates take two significant measures. First, they immediately suspended the forced sales of goods carried out by the corregidores, the cause of one of the main indigenous outcries throughout the Andes. Second, and more important in the short term, they launched extensive preparations for war. They called up the urban militias, requested that Viceroy Juan José de Vértiz immediately dispatch companies from the regular Spanish army in Buenos Aires, and instructed all the provincial corregidores to organize military forces in their respective districts.

For the Andean peoples in northern Potosí, the massive recruitment of troops confirmed their worst fears: soldiers would be sent to the province to avenge their bloody assault on the Spanish militias in the town of Pocoata. But as they had warned in the letter that they forced corregidor Alós to write from his jail cell in Macha, any attack on them would only escalate the conflict. Indeed, from early September on, the region was turning into a theater of operations. Facing the prospect of an imminent punitive expedition, the peasants stockpiled maize, salted meat, coca leaves, and slings in strategic locations. People entering the province were thoroughly searched, and all correspondence was intercepted. Men were sent to neighboring provinces to coordinate military assistance; the communities of Condocondo (Paria province) and Tinquipaya (Porco province) patrolled the area so that they could warn of the arrival of Spanish troops. Armed with slings, whips, and clubs, the Indians guarded the main ravines and passageways connecting Chayanta province to Chuquisaca. It was said that the peasants were determined to ambush the soldiers "in the narrow passes and mountain terrain" before they could reach their towns; they boasted that two columns of fifteen hundred Indians would be waiting for the troops the moment they set foot in the province.

But there was something much more significant than these preparations for war (which, in any case, would never be put into practice, since the Spanish army would not enter Chayanta until many months later, after the rebellion had already been put down). The widespread political unrest provoked, to paraphrase the anthropologist James C. Scott, a deroutinization of everyday life in which the normal categories through which social reality is apprehended no longer applied (Scott 1985: 333). What was at stake was the set of social relationships that had molded the existence of the native population for centuries. Violence against caciques soon spread throughout the power structure in the countryside.

This is what Katari was alluding to when he warned, in a letter sent to the Audiencia in early September, that the grievances of the Indian communities should be redressed without delay, since "only thus may their daily and continual uprisings be calmed, which are very detrimental to His Majesty because they are *occupied and perverted in these revolutions*" (Serulnikov 2003: 162, emphasis added).

One of these many revolutions took place in the town of Sacaca. There the communities pursued, beat, and removed their caciques from office, and then expropriated their rich farmland, mills, and cattle. The Sacaca caciques were members of the Ayaviri Cuisara family, one of the most ancient lineages of Andean lords, who had obtained the rare privilege of possessing their own coat of arms in honor of past services to the Crown. Little time passed before the assaults on the ethnic chiefs was extended to the clergy, mestizos, and creoles. When one of the two caciques, Manuel Ayaviri, tried to take refuge in the chapel of Acasio, a village located in a valley where the Sacaca community owned cropland, hundreds of Indians bearing a red flag and armed with stones, slings, and clubs tied up the priest without compunction, stoned the chapel, and threatened to set fire to it. Nor did they hesitate to invade the province of Cochabamba, where their pueblo's other cacique, Phelipe Ayaviri, had taken refuge. (A few months later, as we will see, Cochabamba would become the setting for some of the bloodiest attacks on the Hispanic population.) In the town of Sacaca itself, the Indians dragged the parish priest's assistant out of the church for helping the cacique to escape, tied him up, and set a crown of thorns on his head as a sign of humiliation. The town dwellers did not have any better luck. In an open rejection of the established social hierarchies, the rebels forced any creoles and mestizos who hadn't already fled to wear indigenous clothing; the Indians then went through the pueblo streets shouting insults at them and throwing stones at their houses.

In the valley of San Pedro de Buena Vista, too, struggles between communities and their caciques quickly carried over into other social realms. The rebels demanded that their priest, Joseph de Herrera, the highest church official in the province, hand the caciques under his protection over to them, put the church fee schedule of 1772 (which he had systematically refused to implement) into effect, and exempt Indians from paying tithes and half-tithes, another recurrent peasant complaint over the past few decades.[2] After several violent altercations, on Sunday, September 24, a crowd descended on the town, brandishing their weapons and blowing on their *pututus*, wind instruments made from ox horns that were used to call community members to meeting. The main leader, an Indian from the Sicoya community named Simón Castillo, publicly confronted the priest in the village square. His honor wounded, Herrera slapped Castillo and had him placed under arrest. A pitched battle then broke out in which the Spanish residents opened fire on the crowd. The massiveness and fierceness of the assault eventually forced the Spanish to lock themselves inside the church. The crowd then attacked the church for several hours, until Simón Castillo was set free and Herrera acceded to their demands. The insurgent communities took complete control of the town, sacking its creole and mestizo residents' empty houses. Since the village of San Pedro was situated in one of the most fertile valleys in the province, many of its dwellers were large landowners. Little wonder, then, that the challenges to the local power structures quickly encompassed challenges to land property rights. The Indians invaded some of the haciendas in the valley, swearing "that the Spaniards cannot have any possessions"; one parish priest noted that someone had "published a decree establishing that the owners of the haciendas in that district had to go away and turn over the lands to the Indians of the community" (Serulnikov 2003: 169). Other rural areas dominated by private landholdings met similar fates during the ensuing months.

By September 1780, the rebellion had taken on a distinctively regional scope. In the province of Paria, the communities of Condocondo, Toledo, Challacollo, and Challapata rose up against their ethnic lords. The case of Condocondo is particularly significant, for this community had figured in one of the most violent revolts of the years preceding the

2. The tithe (*diezmo*) was a tax of 10 percent on all crops and newborn cattle of European origin, payable to the bishop, who generally farmed collection out to non-Indian tax collectors. Non-European crops such as potatoes and quinoa were exempt, but European products (wheat, barley, pigs, chickens, and so on) made up a larger proportion of Indian agricultural production over the centuries. When grown by Indians on community land, these products were supposed to be subject to a half-tithe (*veintena*), a tax of 5 percent, but tax collectors often tried to charge the full tithe anyway, in addition to overcharging and cheating in other ways.

rebellion: in 1774, the Indians had executed their caciques, Gregorio and Andrés Llanquipacha, a family of ethnic lords similar in profile to Florencio Lupa. The Condocondo Indians owned cropland in several zones of the province of Chayanta, and they enjoyed close relationships with many communities there. Hence Katari and the Machas had repeatedly petitioned the Audiencia to free those who had been sentenced for executing the Llanquipachas; these prisoners were in fact quickly released during the wave of panic that followed the discovery of Florencio Lupa's head on a cross in the outskirts of Chuquisaca. Before returning to Condocondo, the released prisoners visited Katari in Macha. Many other Indians from Paria province made the same journey. The corregidor of the province, Manuel de la Bodega y Llano, lamented the fact that "[Tomás Katari] is the oracle whom the natives of these provinces consult about their doubts and questions" (Serulnikov 2003: 183). He was right to lament it. As we will see, in January 1781, after the death of Katari, Bodega himself would be executed by the Indians of his province.

In Porco province, an ayllu of the community of Tinquipaya whose territories bordered on those of Macha was the first to attack its cacique. The Indians of the community of Coroma, also in Porco province, followed Katari's advice and replaced their cacique with one "of their entire confidence," then proceeded to deliver their tribute directly to the royal treasury in Potosí, as the Machas had done and as their neighbors in Pocoata had done before them years earlier. When their new cacique was arrested in Potosí, he explained that the communities were obeying an Indian from another community, and another province for that matter, because "among the Indians it is known that Katari had brought some rulings that benefited them, especially regarding repartos; and for this reason everybody respects him and views him as superior" (Serulnikov 2003: 183).

The political role assumed by Tomás Katari represented a profound subversion of colonial power relationships. Since his return to the province, he had become a middleman between the Andean peoples and the Spanish rulers. At this point in time, among the native communities of Chayanta and, as we have just seen, of other provinces as well, there was no source of authority higher than his. The reaction of the colonial elites to this sudden collapse of the natural order of things was vividly illustrated in a letter that the priest of Sacaca sent Katari in mid-October. After swearing vengeance for the assaults on the clergy and the other non-Indian residents, he warned: "Look to what you are doing! Fear God! For you are mortal and when you least expect it He will take your life and send you to hell for all eternity." In the meantime, he asked Katari to let him know

> how I am to address you in the future (for I desire your communica-
> tion and correspondence), whether as Your Majesty, or as Your Ex-
> cellence, or as Your Lordship, in order that I might not err, for I am
> ignorant of everything, and know only that I am suffering in your
> name, and everyone in our parish and the priests in all the parishes
> in the valley are suffering, and I anticipate your response because it
> would not be proper for a man of your fine qualities not to reply.
> (Serulnikov 2003: 171)

The sarcasm reflects the profound anxiety brought about by the abrupt demise of colonial social hierarchies in the Andean villages. Katari, let us recall, was not only a member of native society; he was also an Indian commoner, illiterate, poor, a mere peasant like the thousands of other peasants who at that moment were defying their local overlords—secular and religious, indigenous and Spanish. Katari, for his part, delivered the tribute from several Indian communities to the royal treasury (thus ful-filling his promise to favor the Crown's interests) and dispatched dozens of letters to the colonial magistrates—including the viceroy of Río de la Plata and the king himself—in which he presented himself as a humble subject. But he did so from a singularly peculiar position of power: as the highest authority in the region. Not for nothing, the interim corregidor who had been chosen to replace Joaquín Alós, Juan Antonio de Acuña, warned Katari that no matter how many economic and symbolic gestures of subservience to the Crown he might display, to receive "Indians from other provinces who come to the town of Macha to pay him obedience as if he was sovereign . . . was a extremely grave crime because it amounted to usurping the right to the Sovereign" (Serulnikov 2003: 179). Katari never showed signs of aspiring to such a right, but he did let Spanish rulers know that if the legitimate claims of the Andean peoples were not addressed, "the Kingdom will be lost" (Serulnikov 2003: 184).

And that is exactly what happened. In late November 1780, on secret orders sent by the Audiencia of Charcas, Tomás Katari was finally ambushed and taken prisoner. Manuel Álvarez Villarroel, the militia commander from the mining town of Aullagas, the last bastion of the Hispanic population in Chayanta province, arrested him along with his scribe and a few other collaborators when the indigenous leader was in the countryside collecting the tribute from his community. Perhaps because at that time of year most Indians were out sowing their fields in the valley, there was no immediate reaction to the arrest. It quickly became obvious, however, that a massive assault on the mining town was inevitable. The first week of January 1781, as the situation in Aullagas was growing untenable, Acuña decided to conduct Katari personally to Chuquisaca. Though he tried to get to the city along small bypaths, while he and his tiny entourage were passing through a narrow gorge near the village of Quilaquila in Yamparáez province on January 8, they were intercepted by a large crowd of Indians from both Yamparáez and Chayanta. After the first skirmish, finding himself in a desperate situation, Acuña pushed Katari off a cliff. In response, the Indians stoned him and his soldiers to death. As had been done after other battles, their bodies were stripped naked and left unburied as a sign of their bestial nature. The corregidor also had his eyes removed; one of the attackers explained "that in this way they had him taken by the Devils" (Serulnikov 2003: 185).

The remains of Tomás Katari were carried to a nearby hamlet. All that night the people who had taken part in the combat kept vigil over his body. His feet were still bound in the shackles that had been locked onto them for the march to Chuquisaca. The Indians drank chicha (corn beer) and performed a set of rituals that the contemporary sources, to our dismay, described only as "superstitions." But their attachment to their own religious practices does not mean that the Indians did not consider themselves Catholic. They were indeed Catholic in their own way, just as they were the king's subjects in their own way, and peasants in their own way. The next day they bore Katari's body to the small village of Quilaquila so that he, unlike his enemies, could be given a Christian burial by the priest in the church cemetery.

Katari's burial might have been Christian. But what it meant to be a true Christian, and to whom the kingdom of this world belonged, were issues to be settled in the coming days. Five weeks after the funeral, numerous indigenous communities from all over the region were encamped on the outskirts of the city of Chuquisaca, threatening to exterminate its entire population. The multitude of Indians whom the city dwellers had thought they had seen alongside the severed head of the cacique Lupa in September 1780 had now become a reality.

8

The Road to Chuquisaca

Over the course of five weeks from the death of Tomás Katari to the siege of Chuquisaca, the indigenous rebellion was transformed under the leadership of his brothers Dámaso and Nicolás into an anticolonial war.[1] To avenge their leader's fate, the Indians organized a massive assault on the mining town of Aullagas, the main Spanish stronghold within Chayanta province. As Manuel Álvarez Villarroel, a mine owner and the militia commander of Aullagas, managed to relay in his final letter, "Nothing is being voiced but this: *since our king Katari is dead, let's all die killing*" (Serulnikov 2003: 189). After several hard battles, Álvarez Villarroel was handed over to the rebels by his own mine workers. In the presence of Nicolás Katari, he was beaten to death and then decapitated. In the ensuing weeks, the same fate befell many other enemies of the Andean peoples—former caciques, tax collectors, a few hacienda owners. Physically eliminating enemies had by then become an accepted insurgent practice.

1. Historical information and analysis in this section draw on Serulnikov 2003: 186–214.

In the opening weeks of 1781, the regional dimension of the uprising took hold. In some of their letters Dámaso and Nicolás Katari began to identify themselves with political titles such as "Captain Major of the Province of Charcas" and "Governor and Representative [*Apoderado*] of all communities," which indicated the broadened scale of the movement. Accordingly, both leaders were said to have appointed ethnic authorities at the request of several communities of Chayanta and neighboring provinces, declared the abolition of old colonial burdens such as tithes, half-tithes, first fruits, and alcabalas, and called for joint resistance to the Spanish forces.[2] Nicolás, for example, called for the communities of Yocalla and Tarapaya, near Potosí, to "put in all the effort you can muster . . . for that is what we are doing here for our own part, hearing the rumors of soldiers marching from all the large Pueblos such as Chuquisaca, Potosí, and other places . . . and considering this, you must exert yourselves most diligently to prevent these soldiers from advancing, because if these soldiers advance they will finish us off, so do as you wish according to your wills" (Serulnikov 2003: 192–193). The Indians of Yocalla in fact did write a defiant note around this time to the governor of Potosí.

Meanwhile, in Paria province, the Indians of the community of Challapata executed their corregidor, Manuel de la Bodega y Llano. Over the preceding years the forced sale of goods and the corregidor's collusion with the caciques had provoked repeated clashes. In late 1780, as the rebellion gained momentum, Bodega sought refuge in Oruro, but when he realized that the proceeds from the reparto would be lost, he decided to return to Paria province, escorted by a contingent of some eighty soldiers. It was a fateful decision. On his arrival in the pueblo of Challapata on January 15, he arrested all the community authorities, including cacique Mariano Lope Chungara and alcalde Santos Mamani—two men who, as we will soon see, would end up playing central roles in the

2. First fruits (*primicias*): another ecclesiastical tax, in principle consisting of the first offspring of farm animals and the first half-bushel or so of grains harvested each year; customary practices varied widely, but in many areas primicias devolved into a kind of head tax, leveled only on peasants, to support the parish priest. In some places, primicias were presented to the priest in the form of baskets of agricultural goods, in elaborate annual ceremonies; in others, they became a cash payment and their collection was farmed out along with that of tithes and alcabalas.

confrontations to come. It took only a few hours for the Spanish militias to be completely overwhelmed by the Indian masses. Some ten soldiers lost their lives; the rest, including the corregidor, had to seek refuge in the church. The rebels then threatened to set fire to the church building and execute everyone inside it if Bodega was not handed over immediately. Fearing the worst, the corregidor walked out, surrounded by clergy, and on bended knees "with great humility and tears he begged all the Indians to forgive him and he likewise forgave them everything they owed for repartos" (Cajías de la Vega 2004: 503). The Indians had no use anymore for this type of absolution. Bodega was dragged into the village's central square and, on the rebels' instructions, beheaded by his own domestic slave. The same fate befell the corregidor of Carangas province, Mateo Ibáñez de Arcos, whose abuse of the forced sale of goods system had given rise to constant complaints since his assumption of the office in 1775. He was besieged in the town of Colque and, on January 26, captured and executed. All of these incidents put the provinces of the southern Andes on a war footing. Fearing they would be attacked by rebel forces, the mestizo and Spanish residents fled to the nearest cities. For their part, the peasant communities effectively took control of the countryside and hastened their preparations for the inevitable battles to come.

This process of regional expansion and political radicalization culminated in the siege of Chuquisaca by tens of thousands of Indians from various provinces. Chuquisaca was the oldest city in Upper Peru and the seat of the three most prominent colonial institutions: the Audiencia of Charcas, the university, and the archbishopric. As we will see later, another important city in the region, the mining town of Oruro, would also be the seat of a successful uprising. It is quite unlikely that the assault on Chuquisaca would have occurred without the Tupamarista uprising in Cusco, but the links between the two events resist simplification. Although there is no evidence of direct contacts between the two movements, it is clear that news of Túpac Amaru and the circulation of some of his edicts exercised a powerful influence in the region. In Paria province, for example, it was reported that as the Indians of Challapata marched the severed head of corregidor Bodega through the streets, they proclaimed that they were going to offer it to their Inca king. Though no causal relationship existed between the two rebellions, Túpac Amaru did offer the southern Andean communities a seemingly viable political alternative, a powerful emblem that could be opposed to a social order in apparent disarray. A native, indigenous king could replace a powerless, too-distant Spanish monarch. In his final testimony before his execution, Nicolás Katari neatly summed up this conjunction of local insurgency and neo-Inca symbolism: he recalled that the Indians of Chayanta province,

> trusting to the protection of other provinces they had called to join them, believed themselves capable of keeping their resolutions, which would yield many benefits; and as the news of Túpac Amaru reached them at this time and they were told he had been crowned as king, the new enthusiasm emerged of recognizing him as such and offering him their allegiance, never doubting that they would remain under his dominion, with fewer hardships, if they managed to finish off all the Spaniards. (Serulnikov 2003: 188)

What did "fewer hardships" mean? His brother Dámaso spelled it out this way during his final interrogation:

> That in every way the government had to change. That it should be fair, benign, and free of levies; and in gratitude for the well-being they expected, and for having a native king, they wished to await him by conquering this city, placing it and the allegiance of all the Indians who should populate it at his feet; and with his arrival they expected to redeem themselves from fees, duties, repartos, tithes, and first fruits, and to live without the cares that these taxes place upon them, being at last the lords of their own lands and of the fruits they produce, in peace and tranquility. (Serulnikov 2003: 197)

Here Dámaso Katari described a peasant utopia infused with a nativist utopia. And even so, the fusion of local experiences of confrontation with the great messianic expectations awakened by the Tupamarista revolution was a more conflictive process than these retrospective statements might suggest. The siege of Chuquisaca by indigenous communities from several surrounding provinces represented the greatest challenge to Spanish domination in the history of the region. But it doesn't seem that the insurgent forces had any concrete plans to "conquer the city," as Dámaso later put it, and the explicit objectives of the siege continued to be intimately linked to the conflict's local history. On February 13, some seven thousand men and women encamped on a nearby hill named La Punilla (the total population of Chuquisaca at the time was no more than eight thousand). They then sent letters to the Audiencia in which they vowed to attack the city and use the ministers' skulls as cups for drinking *aloja*[3] if those officials did not respond to their demands (Serulnikov 2003: 197). But all they were demanding was for the Audiencia to return the documents that Acuña had confiscated from Tomás Katari and to free some Indians from Quilaquila who had been arrested for their role in killing their corregidor. There are no signs that they tried to negotiate terms of occupation for the city, as Túpac Amaru did in the siege of Cusco, or as Túpac Katari would later do in the much more protracted assault on La Paz.

On February 18, after the failure of a disorganized first attempt to dislodge the Indian forces from La Punilla, the Charcas authorities finally decided to dispatch two priests to parley with the Indians, having them bring copies of the documents that Tomás Katari had obtained on his journey to Buenos Aires in 1779 and an offer of a general amnesty. The reaction to this proposal reveals the deep ambiguities underlying the insurgent movement. For one thing, the copies of the documents didn't include all the items the Indians had requested. But much more importantly, the documents themselves must have already seemed irrelevant to many of the insurgents, vestiges of an era that was coming to an end: what else could the presence of thousands of armed Indians on the outskirts of the ancient city mean? Dámaso later recalled that "such was the repugnance and resistance felt by many, and in particular by the Indian women, that, under coercion and fearing the loss of life, it was resolved to remain at our post and not assent to the emissaries' admonitions." Yet their ambivalence about the goals of the siege did not disappear. Dámaso again insisted that the communities "are expecting the favorable papers that my brother got from my Lord the Viceroy, for they include the papers about the Clerical Fees, and about the Repartos and Alcabala that have been abolished, and it was for that reason that my brother's life was taken." He then concluded: "Moreover, I warn you that

3. *Aloja* is a fermented drink brewed from *algarrobas*, the seeds of a tree related to mesquite.

we are tributaries of the King Our Lord" (Serulnikov 2003: 198). That these ambiguities were not merely rhetorical is shown by the fact that at least one large group of Indians from Chayanta, the rebellious community of Moromoro, whose members had joined the siege after executing their cacique and attacking their town's Spanish dwellers, decided to accept the authorities' offer; in response to the proclamation of a general amnesty, they retreated en masse from La Punilla.

These vacillations proved catastrophic. On February 20, two days after this odd attempt at negotiation, three columns of 750 militiamen from the city commenced a second and more coordinated assault on rebel positions. The Indians attempted to resist the onslaught, but there was little they could do against well-organized and well-armed troops that were resolved to do battle this time. The following account by a Spanish witness of the attack reflects once more the consequences of a clash between stones and bullets:

> After they realized that all their stones were not enough to hinder the advance . . . they no longer cared about their defense but only about saving their lives, and they gave over to a headlong rush from the field: so that, like a troop of Sheep, they poured out across the entire Hill, endeavoring to hide among the rocks and crags of the earth, where at their leisure our men cut down all those who were slow to flee from their hands, bloodying their blades even on the wretched women. More than three hundred Indians were left dead on the field, apart from many wounded who later on would die in the surrounding area. (Serulnikov 2003: 198–199)

The debacle of the siege of Chuquisaca had ominous consequences for the future of the indigenous movement: it undermined the leadership of the Katari brothers, weakened the Indian communities' confidence in the feasibility of the whole enterprise, and exacerbated internal strife within Andean society. The implications of all this shortly became plain. But in the meantime, commitment to radical insurgency outlasted this military debacle. To begin with, resisting the Spanish troops had become a matter of survival. When Dámaso Katari was on his way back to Macha, some Indians "begged him—since it was normal for soldiers to pursue everyone, advancing to kill them and consume their cattle and property—to make every effort to resist the soldiers with as many people as possible" (Serulnikov 2003: 199). Furthermore, at this point news began to arrive about a new focal point of rebellion. This uprising was led not by Indians but by the creole elites. It was centered in an urban area, not the rural world; in fact, it was the first rebel movement that succeeded in putting an important city under insurgent control. And it had been carried out in the name of Túpac Amaru. The news about this event, the Oruro rebellion, reached the residents of Chuquisaca as they were celebrating their victory in La Punilla. For good reason, their celebration gave way to deep dismay.

9

....

Creole Tupamaristas

The execution of corregidor Manuel Bodega y Llano in the town of Challapata, Paria province, can be seen as part of the wave of social upheaval
that was embracing the whole Charcas region, and as the culmination of
years of local conflicts between Indian communities and rural authorities.[1] But it was also the beginning of something new. The dramatic
events of Challapata caused a tremendous uproar in the provincial capital, the small mining town of Poopó, which provided most of the soldiers
who had accompanied the corregidor. The residents of Poopó, like many
other creoles and mestizos in Paria, feared that the insurgents would
come after them next. Besides, until then workers in the silver mines and
processing mills had not collaborated much with the rebellious peasants,
but as in other zones of the Andes they now began to take advantage of
the state of widespread political unrest to settle old scores with their
bosses. The priest of Poopó recounted that the mine laborers "gathered
with bugles, drums, and slings and with their racket and din they caused
everyone the greatest dismay, breaking doors, robbing houses, stripping

1. Historical information and analysis in this section draw on Cajías de la Vega 2004.
The section is also based on Lewin 1957; Robins 2002; and Cornblit 1995.

and beating everyone they could catch" (Cajías de la Vega 2004: 509). Despite the grimness of the situation, many of the town's most powerful individuals—the mine owners and local merchants—did not limit themselves to raising a militia company, asking the Audiencia for instructions, or simply fleeing to the nearby city of Oruro, where almost all of them had houses, relatives, and associates. Those who stayed in Poopó instead decided to hold an assembly and name a replacement for Bodega on their own authority—someone, they said, who would be able to appease the agitated spirits of the peasants and mine workers. That man was Juan de Dios Rodríguez.

Rodríguez was the largest mine and mill owner in Paria province and Oruro. A colonel in the militia and a member of one of the most traditional local families, he and his renowned brother Jacinto were also the leading figures of a group of creoles of Oruro who had been at loggerheads with the Peninsulars for years over the command of local power structures. The Rodríguez brothers, along with two other prominent Oruro families, the Herreras and Galleguillos, had monopolized the major positions in the town council (cabildo), a traditional body of municipal self-government. As in all Spanish American cities, some of these offices were purchased for life from the Crown, and others, like the high post of alcalde ordinario, were elected by the town council members every January 1. The other important institution of local government, the post of corregidor (a royal official appointed directly by the king), had also been under control of local families for most of the eighteenth century. But in 1781, things took a new turn. The appointment of a Basque man named Ramón de Urrutia as corregidor of Oruro changed the traditional balance of power between Peninsulars and creoles. Since his arrival in 1779, Urrutia had endeavored by every means possible to sideline the Rodríguez brothers and their allies in town government—in his own words, "so that the vara [the ornamental staff symbolizing the alcalde's office] might depart from the house of the Rodríguez brothers, who were trying to keep it forever" (Cajías de la Vega 2004: 480).

In January 1781, Urrutia finally achieved his goal. He imposed his own candidates in the wake of contested town council elections. Most of the positions, including those of alcalde, ended up in the hands of Peninsulars or creoles aligned with the corregidor. Reactions came swiftly. Most of the creole elites and the urban plebeians of Oruro boycotted the customary public celebrations after the elections, in particular the thanks-giving mass and the bullfight. For several days, Rodríguez even refused to turn over the alcalde's vara. Rumors spread of a popular riot against the interloping *chapetones* (outsiders or foreigners); even more alarm-ingly, the streets of Oruro were festooned with pasquinades that associ-ated the current upheaval with a supposed adherence to the Tupamarista uprising. One of these lampoons spoke, in obvious allusion to Túpac Amaru, of "shaking off the yoke of the foreign king, and crowning the rightful owner," and also of "killing the despotic ministers" (Lewin 1957: 565). In *ancien régime* societies, where making opinions public was a privilege to be granted by the king and his magistrates, putting out anonymous pasquinades and handbills was the main mechanism for expressing political dissidence. Nobody took their content lightly.

After his defeat in the council elections of January 1, 1781, Juan de Dios Rodríguez decided to leave Oruro for his house in Poopó. Thus, when the corregidor of Paria, Manuel Bodega y Llano—another Peninsu-lar corregidor, just like Urrutia—was executed barely a week later, and immediately afterward the residents of Poopó rushed to elect Rodríguez as his replacement, the Spanish officials and their allies thought they were witnessing the confirmation of their worst fears: a coalition of creoles and Tupamaristas. They were partly right and partly wrong. As we saw above, the indigenous revolt in Challapata followed its own dynamic and was linked with other community protest, past and present, in Paria itself and in the surrounding provinces. It was by and large unrelated to the aspirations and grievances of the creole aristocracy. But it is also true that the creoles and mestizos didn't hesitate to take advan-tage of the disturbances to advance their own political agenda: they accused the deceased corregidor of provoking peasant collective vio-lence simply by raking in the cash from his abusive forced sale of goods, and they made sure to replace him with their most prominent represen-tative. It is no surprise, then, that the appointment of Rodríguez was highly praised by the Oruro treasury officials, most of them creoles, but not confirmed by the all-Peninsular ministers of the Audiencia of Char-cas. The local elite groups, in short, may not have been complicit with the indigenous insurrection. Yet, considering how news of the ongoing neo-Inca uprising in Cusco was spreading, and considering that the Andean peoples held complete control over vast rural areas in Paria,

Chayanta, Yamparáez, and Carangas, they had made it all too clear that they were prepared to play with fire.

Why did the radicalism and massiveness of the indigenous rebellion fail to tone down the internal rivalries among the ruling elites in Oruro, as it had in Cusco, Chuquisaca, and other Andean cities? It appears that the hostility between creoles and Peninsulars had deeper roots here and was of longer standing. As early as 1739 the authorities had discovered a conspiracy of creoles and mestizos, supported by a few Indian caciques, aimed at ending Spanish rule. That abortive uprising had been led by a self-proclaimed descendant of the Incas, the creole Juan Vélez de Córdoba. Less spectacularly, but more relevantly in the long run, the acrimony between creoles and Peninsulars was expressed in continual struggles for economic resources, local power, and honor. Oruro's main productive activity, silver mining, was dominated by local families. The great merchants and money-lenders, on the other hand, tended to be Peninsulars. They were the ones who financed the mining activities, extended credit to mine owners so they could purchase mercury (an essential material for extracting silver from raw ore), advanced money and merchandise to corregidores for their repartos, and controlled the long-distance trade with other Andean cities and the viceregal capitals—first Lima, later Buenos Aires. The mining business could sometimes be very profitable, but it was subject to steep fluctuations. When the mining sector entered a phase of acute stagnation in the 1770s, the owners of mines and mills (especially those who had not diversified their investments into haciendas or other commercial undertakings) were increasingly left at the mercy of the great moneylenders. They began to dub these moneylenders advenedizos (upstarts, foreigners) and judíos (Jews) (Cajías de la Vega 2004: 471–472). Hence in the collective imaginary (although not necessarily in practice), occupational differences and the resulting conflicts of interest became associated with people's birthplaces.

The antagonism between creoles, or "fellow countrymen" (that is, people born in the town or assimilated into local society), on the one hand, and Peninsulars, or chapetones (outsiders, regardless of where they were born), on the other, was reflected in disputes over ethnic adscription and honor. Oruro was a town of some six thousand people, roughly one-third the size of Chuquisaca, in which patricians and plebeians shared public space and daily life. To a greater degree here than in other colonial cities, residents had developed common cultural codes governing dress and speech, the generalized use of the Quechua language, the celebration of Carnival, and the forms of entertainment and sociability. The long-standing process of *mestizaje* affected both the phenotypic traits and the cultural practices of the local population. For the urban patriciate, this meant a growing identification with Oruro, their birthplace, their *patria chica*, their homeland; for plebeians, a sense of connection with their superiors. For Europeans and for creoles from other places, the Oruro elites were of low extraction. One creole from Lima, for example, was disturbed by the fact that one of the most distinguished patrician men in Oruro would "show signs of regular life with the uncouth Indians" and would drink and dance "with them wearing their own dress" (Cajías de la Vega 2004: 472). They may have been rich, but their wealth did not redeem them from their mean ancestry and doubtful lineages, their impurity of blood. "*Cholos!*" (assimilated Indians), the outsiders would spit at them, in the frequent bickering that would break out between the two sides on the street. Jacinto Rodríguez himself—a prosperous man, a town council official, and a future corregidor of the city—was the target of this epithet during a squabble with a creole from Lima. Indignant, he called the man who offended him "a rebel, a man who could not tell or discern the difference between the color of a cholo's face and Rodríguez's, which is that of a Spanish man" (Cajías de la Vega 2004: 471).

For the Oruro patricians, therefore, occupying the top posts in the institutions of local government wasn't a matter of power alone; it was also a question of honor, a way of reaffirming their membership the white elite, of defending their legitimate place in the hierarchy of privileges. But in this realm as in the realm of economic activity, their luck began to shift as the cataclysm of 1781 approached. The discrimination against creoles that the Crown had practiced as state policy since the 1750s led to the appointment of Spaniards as corregidores of Oruro and Paria provinces, two posts of great significance for local residents that theretofore had often been held by creoles, including the Rodríguez family. The Peninsular corregidores Urrutia in Oruro and Bodega in Paria (like Alós in Chayanta and Ibáñez in Carangas) were the latest examples of this trend. The highest regional court, the Audiencia of Charcas, whose magistrates and prosecutors had all been creoles not many years before, was also now dominated by Spaniards. Town government was the last important bastion that the Oruro aristocracy had left, thus the triumph of the European party in the council elections of January 1781 was the last straw.

The protracted social and political antagonisms that had fostered the conformation of two opposing parties made the Oruro conflict the sole genuinely creole revolt in all the Andean area during the Tupamarista revolution. This does not mean that there was direct contact between the Cusco and Oruro rebel leaderships. As far as we know, there was no such contact. According to historian Boleslao Lewin, the only attempted communication between them came in a letter sent by Andrés Mendigure Túpac Amaru to the Oruro creoles in September 1781, many months after the mining town had already gone over to the royalist side (Lewin 1957). But the two events that finally broke the relationship between the Peninsular and creole factions in Oruro—the town council elections and the execution of the corregidores of Paria and Carangas—coincided with the widespread circulation of a series of edicts and proclamations that Túpac Amaru had issued during his march through the provinces of the Collao. Those pronouncements, as already mentioned, called on Indians and creoles to join forces against their common enemy, the Spanish rulers. In Cusco and the Collao, these exhortations yielded modest results at best. Oruro was a different matter. For the patrician aristocracy, the neo-Inca movement offered the chance to place their old frustrations and longings in a new context. For the Spanish magistrates and Peninsular elites, it crystallized the notion that the Oruro creoles, due to their cultural traits and political leanings, were closer to the colonized than to the colonizers. The creole ambivalence toward the early outbreaks of Indian rebellion in Paria and the social prejudices of the Peninsulars nurtured a climate of mutual distrust that raised the intraelite conflict to extremes without precedent or parallel. It also pushed Oruro's miners, hacienda owners, merchants, and city officials to pursue an alliance with urban plebeians and indigenous peasants that would have been hard to imagine just a few weeks earlier.

Let's examine this process. After the corregidores of the neighboring provinces of Paria and Carangas were murdered in late January and the violence raged on throughout Chayanta and Yamparáez, the Oruro residents started preparing to resist an imminent invasion of indigenous forces. As in all the towns and cities in the region, several militia companies were organized immediately. But in Oruro the militia itself became the heart of the conflict. Over the years, the Oruro creoles had been acquiring the top posts in the militia regiments, just as they had done with town council positions. Since 1770, Juan de Dios Rodríguez and his brother Jacinto Rodríguez had attained the highest ranks in the local militia—colonel and lieutenant colonel, respectively. Other mine owners had also acquired the ranks and titles of captain and lieutenant. Nevertheless, when corregidor Urrutia formed four companies of whites and mestizos and one company of slaves—some four hundred militiamen, all told—he placed European officials with close ties to himself at the head of three of those companies. The creoles took this move as a flagrant affront to their honor. One creole captain, for example, on the occasion of a town council meeting, stated that Urrutia "named Europeans from his faction to be captains and other officers, in disrespect of all other patriots whose titles have been confirmed by His Excellence" (Cajías de la Vega 2004: 522). His Excellence, the Buenos Aires viceroy, was then warned that "*from this new invention of outsider* [that is, Peninsular] *grenadiers, with preference over the town dwellers, there may someday follow riotous disturbances*" (Cajías de la Vega 2004, emphasis in original).

That day was not long in coming. When the Oruro militia troops were quartered in early February, rumors of mutual betrayal spread like wildfire. The circulation of Tupamarista decrees favorable to the creoles, and especially the attitude of the Poopó residents toward the execution of corregidor Bodega, made the Europeans suspect that the patricians and plebeians would join forces with the indigenous rebels when the hour of truth arrived. As one resident put it, "The Europeans were publicly proclaiming that the creoles of Oruro had handed General Bodega over to the Indians in Challapata, and they assumed the same thing would happen to them whenever the Indians invaded the Town" (Cajías de la Vega 2004: 523). The creoles, for their part, were convinced that the Peninsulars would wipe them out before that could happen, either doing the deed themselves or having the black soldiers under their command do it for them. These mutual fears of betrayal, though not necessarily well founded, turned into a self-fulfilling prophecy. The corregidor took the first step in this direction by distributing firearms and knives to the Europeans and the slaves but not to the company of creoles and mestizos. The response to this act was immediate. On the night of February 9, the women, children, and relatives of the creole soldiers surrounded the building that served as quarters for the five companies, shouting that the locals were going to be massacred by their peers. They brought sticks, stones, and a few firearms. The militiamen abandoned the barracks, refusing to spend the night unarmed and locked inside with the other companies. One of the leaders of the mutiny and the subsequent general uprising, Sebastián Pagador, a man of modest resources employed by the Rodríguez family, reportedly warned his "friends, fellow countrymen, and comrades" that "the most perfidious treachery against us at the hands of the chapetones" was in progress. He called on them to sacrifice their lives "in defense of the Homeland (la Patria), turning all the humility and submissiveness with which we have up to now borne the chapetones' treachery into wrath and frenzy, in order to cut them to pieces and do away, if it is possible, with that accursed race" (Cajías de la Vega 2004: 548–549).

After a night fraught with threats and rumors, the militiamen refused to return to the barracks. They went instead to Jacinto Rodríguez's house to ask him, as a lieutenant colonel, to intercede with the corregidor. But Rodríguez, displaying a suspicious passivity, did nothing. Nor did the militiamen go back to their quarters. The town became embroiled in a general debate. The militiamen and the plebeians gathered in the main plaza and the popular neighborhoods, more engrossed now in the likelihood of an armed clash with Europeans than in the potential indigenous assault that had given rise to the formation of militias in the first place. Aware that tensions were about to explode, corregidor Urrutia ordered his officers to persuade the creoles that the rumors were utterly false. He went to the main square in person to convince the mutineers that nothing would happen to them. He even offered to spend the night in their quarters to reassure them that nobody would attack them. But it was already too late to ward off the inevitable. At dusk, the sound of bugles, drums, and shouting began to be heard in a popular neighborhood and from a nearby hill named Conchupata. At first people thought it was the long-awaited invasion of Indians, but it turned be the Oruro plebeians themselves. Who were they? Many were mine workers—a large and determined group, mainly indigenous in origin, who endowed the revolt with a level of organization that would be hard to match in cities that lacked such a cohesive social agent. Others came from the motley world of lower classes found in any colonial city: craftsmen and journeymen of various sorts (shoemakers, silversmiths, carpenters, and so on), retail shopkeepers, street vendors, domestic servants, and people without any fixed employment. They were termed "the people," "the plebeians," or "the cholos." Typical of every popular revolt of the time, women participated on an equal footing with men. It was the revolt of an entire community, not of any specific occupational group.

When the patrician militiamen understood the source of the disturbances, they refrained from responding. One hour later the riot turned into a pitched battle. The European officers and militiamen, realizing that the growing riot was aimed at them, opened fire to disperse the crowd. But they were the ones forced to retreat, under a hail of stones hurled by the people. The disturbance soon spread all over town. Streets and plazas turned into battlefields. A minor squabble between a creole militiaman and a Peninsular militiaman was all it took to make the pressure that had been building up for weeks burst forth: the armed locals, instead of trying to contain the rioters, just joined the crowd. The city was then left at the rebels' mercy. Seeing how desperate their predicament was, corregidor Urrutia, the alcaldes, and the top European officers and inhabitants fled that very night to Cochabamba. Those who stayed sought refuge in the churches or the houses of their fellow chapetones and prominent creoles, many of them hauling their valuables with them. That was the case with a rich Spanish merchant named José de Endeiza, whose house on the central plaza became one of the Spaniards' main refuges. At some point the crowd began to set fire to houses. Several Europeans and their slaves were massacred when they tried to escape burning buildings. The violence against individuals was followed by mass looting of houses and shops belonging to chapetones and their allies. Countless gold objects, silver bars, items of wrought silver, and other valuables were seized and split up among the attackers. It was said that the assailants got some fifty thousand pesos from the Endeiza house alone. The violence and looting lasted all night long and into the early morning of February 11. All told, some ten Europeans, five blacks, and three creoles died.

The most prominent creoles and militia officers, including the Rodríguez brothers, were not directly involved in these incidents. In a society like Oruro's, where anonymity was impossible, their personal involvement would have been too audacious. On the other hand, they did nothing to stop the slaughter, and, as with the rebellion in Paria province, they turned out to be its main beneficiaries. On the morning of February 11, a group went to see Jacinto Rodríguez at his house to ask him, as lieutenant colonel in the militia and senior member of the town council, to take charge of the government in view of the political vacuum left by the flight of corregidor Urrutia and other city magistrates. Were Rodríguez and his followers aiming to restore order, or, rather, maneuvering to place themselves at the head of the rebellion? This deliberate ambiguity, whether it stemmed from genuine ideological ambivalence, pragmatic caution for what might lie ahead, or both, would color the entire history of the Oruro rebellion. The ceremony that followed, nevertheless, left no doubt regarding the political meaning of the whole affair. Rodríguez and his retinue went straight to the main plaza, where the people were already gathered. From the balcony of the town hall he admonished the crowd to submit to the high authorities, and asked them "whether they wished to recognize Don Jacinto Rodríguez as such authority, to which they replied as one that they acclaimed him head magistrate, and that they would obey him in everything, but they would kill the Corregidor [Urrutia] and any other Europeans they might meet, as their declared enemies" (Lewin 1957: 581). Two days later the town council ratified with all due pomp and ceremony the legitimacy of a power born from popular acclamation.

As for the insurgent Indian communities whose impending invasion had given rise to all these disturbances, they began to stream peacefully into Oruro that very afternoon, February 11. No one did anything to stop them. Some five thousand arrived the first day, and four days later their numbers had grown to fifteen thousand. Most of them came from the neighboring rural areas. This multitude—about twice the size of Oruro's permanent population—occupied the city so that, in their own view of the events, they could help the creoles and mestizos finish off the chapetones. Wasn't that what Túpac Amaru's decrees had called for? On February 11 and the days that followed, the Spaniards who had managed to escape the frenzy of the first riot were pursued and massacred. In his inauguration ceremony as town corregidor, Jacinto Rodríguez had instructed the people not to attack those Spaniards who were married to creole women (by the concepts of the time, such men were considered vecinos, full members of urban society, rather than outsiders). But the insurgents had no patience for these fine distinctions. Barely a handful of chapetones managed to survive. The Indians, together with popular urban groups, did not hesitate even to comb through every church in town, drag the refugees outside, and kill them. One priest recalled that "they did not neglect the most hidden room or nook; they even made [us] open the chests and closets, smashed the ceilings and thumped the floors to find out if they sounded hollow, and sniffed the dirt floors to find out whether any holes had been recently dug in them" (Cajías de la Vega 2004: 663). Knowing that many priests would do everything possible to shelter the Spaniards, this scene was repeated over several days. Roughly thirty Spaniards lost their lives in this way. Here, as in other rebel areas, the Indians did not allow the corpses of their enemies to be buried. The looting, moreover, spread to every house and shop that might contain possessions of the Europeans or their allies. Numerous buildings were set ablaze.

The uprising of the Oruro urban population had originally grown out of a deep-rooted hostility toward Peninsulars and other outsiders. It had been inspired, more vaguely for some groups than for others, by news of the Túpac Amaru insurrection, but its causes were distinctly local, relating to both recent and long-standing feelings of disaffection with colonial government. Now, as successive contingents of rebel Indians came down to the city, the creoles finally saw their revolt turn into a full-blown branch of the Tupamarista revolution. And they didn't like what they saw. At first there were mutual expressions of solidarity between insurgent peasants and the urban patriciate. On February 13, for example, some two thousand Indians from the community of Sora Sora marched into town in formation and to the sound of musical instruments. A parade was organized in their honor, and all of the leading town officials turned out to greet them. The ceremony concluded with public demonstrations of allegiance to Jacinto Rodríguez. They had no reason not to show such allegiance: over the course of the celebration a decree from Túpac Amaru ordering all chapetones to be killed was publicly proclaimed; the royal coat of arms was ripped from the door of the royal treasury office; a witness later testified that after the event, the highest-ranking creoles milled around exchanging views about the advance of the Tupamarista forces. Nevertheless, it soon became evident that the Indians had their own ideas about the revolution's goals. In addition to implacably persecuting the Spaniards and looting their possessions, they began to demand that farming land be transferred to the native communities. Most of the rural towns in the Oruro area, unlike those in Paria, Chayanta, and other provinces, were settled by Indians legally classified as *yanaconas* or *forasteros*, that is, peasant tenant farmers.[2] One essential demand for them was ownership rights over the plots they farmed. The problem was that many of the fields they claimed as theirs belonged to the same wealthy creoles who were supporting, if not leading, the rebellion. A similar dilemma had faced Juan de Dios Rodríguez in Paria province. After being named interim corregidor, he had established close relations with the insurgents, especially with Mariano Lope Chungara, the cacique of the community of Challapata who had been the main force behind the assault on the provincial militias and Bodega's public execution. But to gain the confidence of the rebels, Rodríguez needed to issue formal deeds transferring lands owned by creoles to the Andean peoples. Class conflicts did not dissipate because indigenous communities and local elites shared a common cause: on the contrary, they rose to the surface. Likewise, the Indians who entered Oruro demanded an end to tribute payments and the return of the money they had already paid that year. Hence the royal treasury offices became a prime target of collective violence. What sense did it make to keep the tribute money in the royal treasury when Spanish rule had been overturned? Town authorities were forced to post a permanent guard to protect the silver deposited in the treasury.

Beyond these economic conflicts, the permanent presence of thousands of Indians in the city made the urban patriciate confront face to face the ultimate reality of the Andean insurgent phenomenon. Because for the indigenous communities in arms, the rebellion was not only, or

2. *Yanacona* and *forastero* were legal categories with complicated histories in both Andean and Spanish legal traditions. Unlike pueblos of *indios del común* (Indian commoners), forastero communities did not have legal title to their land. Forastero status was more or less hereditary: the descendants of the Indians who settled in Oruro as forasteros in the 1500s were still legally identified as such two centuries later. Forasteros were obliged to pay rent for their land and higher rates on taxes and tithes; on the other hand, they were exempt from certain tribute and labor obligations imposed on Indian commoners.

even mainly, about Spanish rule; it was aimed at all forms of colonial social hierarchies. At base it was an act of ethnic-cultural defiance, not just a claim to geopolitical sovereignty. It was an anticolonial movement in the deepest sense. It touched on time-honored relationships of power and deference toward people of Hispanic origin, as well as customary forms of social distinction. This radical egalitarian undercurrent manifested itself clearly in certain overt manners, the most spectacular of which was that the city's patricians, both men and women, were forced to dress in Indian attire at all times. The corregidor, alcaldes, town councillors, and all other distinguished creoles and their family members, with the sole exception of the priests, had to wear traditional Andean clothes: ponchos, homespun shirts, and broad, flat hats. Every creole woman had to use the *acsu*, a wrap-around dress worn over all other clothing. Jacinto Rodríguez himself sported an Andean tunic similar to one used by Túpac Amaru. Oruro patricians also had to carry coca pouches, for they were expected to chew coca leaves as the Indians did. Military symbolism was not exempted from this complete inversion of cultural usages: Spanish flags and drums were replaced, according to one witness, "by the beaten rhythm customary among the Indians of this America" (Cajías de la Vega 2004: 677). Similarly, announcements for public meetings were not to be headed by terms such as *paisanos* or *compatriotas* (both meaning "fellow countrymen" and connoting a creole identity) but by the word *comuna* ("community," usually connoting the indigenous population). For their part, the Indians assumed the right to enter patricians' houses, under the pretext that they had to pursue the chapetones, "and they would ask for gifts of silver, alcohol, and coca." In short, it became plain that acknowledging creole political authority by no means entailed recognizing their sociocultural supremacy. After all, the creoles were ruling in the name of one of their own, Túpac Amaru. A contemporary account explained that "the word on the street was that the Inca ordered, and Don Jacinto obeyed" (Lewin 1957: 475).

In Oruro, then, the grand project of the Tupamarista leadership seemed to have materialized at last: all Americans—creoles, mestizos, and Indians—were now brothers under the tutelage of the new Inca. It took less than a week for the Oruro elites to abandon any illusions they may have had about such a project. An incident that took place on February 13 brought the situation to a point of no return. In response to yet another attempt to occupy the royal treasury offices, Sebastián Pagador, the aforementioned leader of the urban plebeians and a close associate of Jacinto Rodríguez, killed one of the attackers. The Indians immediately took Pagador to the corregidor and demanded that he be punished accordingly. Unable to offer Pagador any protection, Rodríguez had him led off to jail. He never made it, however: on the way there he was beaten to death by the enraged Indian crowd. Faced with their patent inability to subdue the insurgents and hoping to exert some measure of control over the city, the creoles tried to persuade the Indians to return to their towns. On February 14 the city magistrates called all of the Indians to a general meeting in a field at the entrance to Oruro. There they thanked them for services rendered and, to convince them to depart, gave one peso to each person present. They had previously extracted twenty-five thousand pesos from the royal treasury—money that the Indians already considered theirs, since it mainly came from their own prior tribute payments. To mollify any bitterness over the fate of the remaining funds (the treasury held at the time some six hundred thousand pesos), Jacinto Rodríguez even went so far as to promise that the silver "was being kept in reserve for the arrival of their King Túpac Amaru" (Lewin 1957: 551). All those present seemed to accept the offering gladly, and the meeting took on a festive air. Nevertheless, only a minority of rebel peasants agreed to go home. The town was under Tupamarista rule, and they were Tupamaristas, so why should they leave? To make matters worse, during the ensuing days, as the shops belonging to Europeans were emptied out, the crowds began attacking the shops of wealthy creoles. It became evident that they would leave the city only by force.

That force was largely supplied by other insurgent Indians. The creoles mobilized the Indians who were genuinely under their command in order to expel the ones who were only nominally loyal to them. Juan de Dios Rodríguez came to Oruro from Poopó accompanied by Lope Chungara, a large number of Indians from Challapata, and other caciques and indigenous leaders whose trust he had managed to gain in the aftermath of the revolt against corregidor Bodega. In the days leading up to this march, he had resorted to land redistributions to dissuade most of the communities in his province from joining the insurgents in Oruro. Now he needed them as a strike force. Once in the city, Juan de Dios Rodríguez first tried to convince the occupiers that Túpac Amaru did not approve of violence against creoles and that if there were any chapetones still left in town, the city residents would deal with them. He was unsuccessful: it was said that one of the Indian leaders rebuked him for attempting "to kick them out with such contempt" (Cajías de la Vega 2004: 730). On February 16, fierce clashes between the two parties broke out, as a result of which rebel peasant forces had finally to leave the town.

The expulsion of the insurgents marked the end of the ephemeral coalition between Indians and creoles. After that moment, the Oruro aristocracy rushed back into the royalist camp. They began by trying to reestablish the social order within the town. They ordered the members of the lower classes to return any objects they had appropriated during the massive looting of shops and houses. To make it perfectly clear that the days of lawlessness were over, they held a procession of penitence and repentance through the streets of the city. During this procession the clergy exhibited the images of saints from their churches. The bodies of the executed Peninsulars, which the Indians had left lying out in the open, were finally given proper burials. When one group of plebeians refused to return what they had stolen, their leader was arrested. When his followers tried to free him, they were repressed ruthlessly, and their leader was publicly executed. It is unknown just how many valuables were returned to those owners who were still alive or to the authorities. In any case, it is clear that the plebeian groups, no longer enjoying the complicity of the patricians and now threatened with accusations of being seditious Tupamaristas, became disciplined once more as the days went by.

Quite the opposite happened in the surrounding countryside. There, no one could discipline the insurgents. After their break with the creole elites, the rebellion in the Oruro region finally began to look like the other uprisings in the southern Andes. On returning to their towns, the Indians killed cacique Lope Chungara and many others who had collaborated with the Rodríguez brothers. The action was led by Santos Mamani, the alcalde who had been imprisoned with Lope Chungara immediately before the revolt against corregidor Bodega. Mamani was to become the top insurgent figure in the region. It was reported that when Lope Chungara tried to collect tribute, "they took his life, saying that those tribute payments should be paid to Túpac Amaru"; Indians called him a "traitor to his community" (Cajías de la Vega 2004: 735). Juan de Dios Rodríguez's silver mills and other properties were burned down. The attacks on the Hispanic population spread all across the countryside around Oruro and in the towns of Paria province, including its capital, Poopó. On March 9, one month after indigenous forces had peacefully entered a town that they considered under Tupamarista control, two Andean communities near Oruro (Paria and Caracollo) and two others in Paria province (Challacollo and Toledo) assaulted the city of Oruro. Other communities, such as Challapata and Sora Sora, had hoped to join the assault but were unable to make it because of logistical problems. The proclaimed goal of the peasants was to exterminate the inhabitants of Oruro, especially the creoles, for betraying the rebellion and collaborating with royalist forces. They were defeated, however, by several militia companies composed of patricians, plebeians, and clergymen. Ten days later they tried it again. An even larger contingent of communities—some five thousand men and women—surrounded the mining town for several days, interrupting the normal supply of provisions. This attack was again frustrated by the effective resistance of the urban militias. Early April saw the third and most determined assault on Oruro. On this occasion it was led by the most bellicose community in the region, Challapata, with Santos Mamani at its head. Though this time the city's defenses seemed to have been breached, the arrival of a company of a thousand militia soldiers from Cochabamba, five days after the siege had begun, managed to overwhelm the rebel army.

This defeat signaled the end of the uprising in the Oruro area. By then, as we will see, many communities in Chayanta and surrounding provinces had begun to go over to the royalist side. The failure of the three assaults on Oruro induced the Indians of that province to attempt to defect as well. They offered to join the fight against the insurgency in exchange for immunity for their past behavior. Town authorities did not let this opportunity slip. Thus the final pacification of the rural areas of Oruro was to a large extent the work of the same Indians who, in the face of their failure to overturn the established order by force, wanted to regain their right to participate in it by collaborating. The main rebel leaders were arrested and brought to Oruro, where sixteen of them, from Challapata, Poopó, Sora Sora, Challacollo, and other insurgent communities, were sentenced to death—Santos Mamani among them. The Indians, for their part, resumed paying tribute and sending mita laborers to Potosí. And, little by little, in small groups, they began to return to Oruro, this time not to place the town under the rule of Túpac Amaru but to sell their agricultural products in its fairs and markets, as they had been doing for centuries.

As for the creoles, their reconciliation with the Peninsulars and their decisive role in the defense of Oruro and the defeat of the Indian uprising earned them the right to rejoin colonial society. In the aftermath of the rebellion, Jacinto Rodríguez was in fact ratified as the town's corregidor by the highest Spanish authorities—a remarkable turn of events for someone who had been anointed corregidor by a popular assembly, had announced decrees from Túpac Amaru, and had proclaimed his allegiance to the new Inca. Many Spaniards and royalist sectors of Upper Peru never forgot, however, that the Oruro creoles had been accomplices in massacring Peninsulars and looting their property, had welcomed the insurgent forces into the town, had promenaded through its streets wearing Andean garb, and had pinned their hopes on the insurrection. In due course, the main heads of the Oruro movement would be called to account for their acts in the tumultuous days of February 1781. In September 1783, responding to insistent demands for justice, the Crown ordered Viceroy Juan José de Vértiz to take effective measures "for the exemplary punishment of the bloodthirsty criminals of Oruro," including Jacinto and Juan de Dios Rodríguez (Cajías de la Vega 2004: 1061). Some twenty wealthy mine owners, merchants, former corregidores, town officials, and priests—the cream of Oruro society—were arrested in 1784, subjected to interrogation and torture in the city of Potosí, and brought under armed guard to Buenos Aires. Some of them died in Potosí, others on the road to the viceregal capital. The rest faced an endless legal process, during which many (including Juan de Dios Rodríguez) would die in prison of various illnesses. In 1795, the top leaders were sentenced to death, their property confiscated, and "perpetual infamy" declared for their children and grandchildren. As for Jacinto Rodríguez, who didn't live long enough to hear the sentence, his body was ordered disinterred from the cemetery of the Bethlehemite hospital in Buenos Aires, decapitated, sent back to Oruro, and dragged through the streets. This part of the sentence does not appear to have been carried out.

10

Radicalized Violence in Upper Peru

The failure of the assault on Chuquisaca on February 20, 1781, would have dire consequences for the movement led by Dámaso and Nicolás Katari.[1] In the short run, however, news of the outbreak of rebellion in Oruro served as a powerful stimulus for spreading the insurrection across the southern Andean provinces. Moreover, during this period the attacks on non-Indian groups and the symbols of colonial power reached the highest levels of radicalization. Barely three days after the debacle of La Punilla, a few Indians from Chayanta traveled to Oruro, where they obtained a copy of an edict signed by Túpac Amaru himself. It proclaimed that "the King our lord Casimiro Inca Túpac Amaru commands most insistently that his subjects be not insulted in any way, and that they live in brotherly fashion as my loyal subjects. And that the Europeans do no business in our kingdom, nor be given entry to it, for they have possessed it for too many years" (Serulnikov 2003: 199). This was possibly the first proclamation of Túpac Amaru that had reached northern Potosí. Several

1. Historical information and analysis in this section draw on Robins 2002 and Serulnikov 2003. The following works were also very useful: Szeminski 1987; and Lewin 1957.

Indians from Paria province also told Dámaso Katari that "the Indians and the creoles, together, had killed all the chapetones in Oruro, where they remained awaiting Túpac Amaru, who was nearby with nearly eight thousand creoles and six thousand Indians, who were killing all the European Spaniards they met on the way." Dámaso recalled that one document from Túpac Amaru had circulated "from hand to hand" and that, "in conference with the Indian leaders of Macha, and in gratitude to their new King, the community agreed to send an express courier to Túpac Amaru, offering him their allegiance and their service" (Serulnikov 2003: 199). It is not evident what the Andean peoples in this area did make of the differential treatment for creoles and Peninsulars, a social distinction that had been all but absent in their prior actions, including the siege of Chuquisaca. But it is clear that Túpac Amaru's pronouncements and the Oruro uprising may have finally allowed the native communities in the Charcas region to situate their own local experiences of contention in a larger political context. Several Indians reportedly told Dámaso Katari that the official rulings his late brother Tomás had gained in the viceregal court "were not needed any more, because they would get amnesty from their new King and would not have to pay taxes or church fees" (Serulnikov 2003: 200). Even more important, news from other rebel areas helped crystallize the notion of a truly pan-Andean insurgency that articulated the events in Cusco and Upper Peru in tangible ways. As a result, in February and March the rural towns across Charcas and Potosí would witness explosions of collective violence that colonial elite groups had never envisioned.

A large focus of insurgent activity emerged during this time in the rich valleys of Cochabamba. This province was one of the hubs of grain production in the Andes and hosted numerous haciendas and indigenous communities. The fuse was lit in the area surrounding the towns of Arque and Colcha, an agricultural and textile-producing zone that served as a gateway from the Cochabamba valleys to the highlands of Chayanta. As we have already seen, Indians from Sacaca invaded this zone in late 1780 to hunt for their caciques. Though Cochabamba Indians had actively collaborated with their Sacaca peers, no important outrages had been committed in the province at the time. Now things took a very different turn. The indigenous communities of Colcha began to occupy the neighboring haciendas—at least eight hacienda owners died during these attacks—and to mobilize the members of the towns of Arque and Tapacarí. Though the insurgents acted in the name of Túpac Amaru, their attacks were aimed at a much broader social segment than the Tupamarista proclamations had called for. Those public statements had been written under social and political circumstances that had little to do with the realities of those who later invoked them, and they were read less as guidelines than as calls to action. On February 21, for example, the rebel forces occupied the town of Colcha, entered its church, and killed all the non-Indian persons who had looked for safe haven there, including women and children. Following a common pattern, dead bodies were left unburied in the church and nearby plaza. Nor was the clergy exempt. Three priests and two of their assistants were executed. One was quartered; another had his tongue ripped out. The Catholic Church had constituted, both metaphorically and literally, the final refuge of colonialism in the rural villages. Until then, church buildings had served as places of sanctuary, and the attachment of the native peoples to Christian rituals proved more enduring than their acquiescence to secular power. Yet, as the clergy consistently sided with rebels' enemies and as projects of social transformation became more sweeping and radical, church ministers and religious symbols were exposed to fierce attacks. Those assaults conveyed a rejection of the role of the priests in society, and perhaps a loss of faith in the power of the Christian God.

The town of Ayopaia witnessed scenes akin to those in Colcha. On February 23, around four hundred people were massacred inside its church. Two days later, the community of Tapacarí, joined by Indians from other regions, executed a similar number of people inside the village church. It was said that after killing them in the choir and altar, the insurgents danced on the bodies of their victims and drank their blood. Since cannibalism is condemned by Andean societies, drinking the blood of Spaniards, creoles, and mestizos—a recurring practice among indigenous rebels—must be interpreted, according to anthropologist Jan Szeminski, as an indication that Indians viewed them as bestial, diabolical beings, as "nonhuman humans." Religious images and objects were taken to the plaza and reduced to ashes. Some children were hurled from the church bell tower. Several white and mestizo women, after witnessing the execution of their husbands and children, were forced to dress as Indian women, chew coca, and become the Indians' servants or slaves. Hundreds of inhabitants from the nearby town of Tarata later met the same fate. The rich haciendas in the Tapacarí, Sacaba, and Clisa valleys were also attacked in the name of Túpac Amaru, and their owners were executed.

The extreme acts of violence and the realization that they were facing a war to the death led the inhabitants of the village of Cochabamba and surrounding towns to enlist in the militias en masse. A high percentage of the province's population was Hispanic and mestizo due to the early expansion of commercial agriculture here. Hence the authorities were able to put together a powerful force of more than a thousand men, which managed to regain control of the region during the first weeks of March. The repression was implacable. Countless Indians were executed, and hundreds of corpses were left to rot along the roads. The Cochabamba soldiers, whose combat skills, fierceness, and penchant for looting became widely known, would later turn into one of the major strike forces in the suppression of the rebellions in the Oruro and La Paz areas.

The Andean peoples south of Potosí also rose up during this period. On February 27, the Indians of Lípez province executed their corregidor and his children; his wife was taken captive and forced to work as a servant. They did not allow the bodies to be buried. In the pueblo of Tupiza, Chichas province, the native communities and the provincial militia under a mestizo sergeant named Luis Laso de la Vega attacked their corregidor, Francisco García de Prado. When the official sought refuge in his house, the rebels set it on fire. The corregidor was then beheaded, and the Indians reportedly drank his blood. De la Vega declared himself governor of the provinces of Chichas, Lípez, and Cinti in the name of Túpac Amaru; several caciques went to Tupiza to swear allegiance to the rebellion. At least one hacienda owner was executed; his head was brought to Tupiza as a trophy. Guanachaca, Tomave, and the mining town of Tolapampa also saw violent uprisings in which several caciques, mine owners, and non-Indian dwellers lost their lives. Similar disturbances occurred in the towns of Yura, Coroma, and Ubina in the neighboring province of Porco. The indigenous communities invoked the names of both Túpac Amaru and Katari to legitimate their actions. In fact, there is evidence that in early March Indians from various provinces arrived in Chayanta seeking instructions. Dámaso Katari dispatched during this period messages to many rebel communities, such as Yura, Tomave, and Tacobamba in Porco, Tupiza in Chichas, and several in Paria. He asked them to be prepared for combat. Prepared they were indeed.

In Chayanta province itself, in the aftermath of the failure of the assault on Chuquisaca, collective actions assumed unprecedented levels of violence. The most spectacular display took place in the village of San Pedro de Buena Vista. We have seen that this valley town, the principal settlement of hacienda owners and other Hispanic residents in the province, had been the focal point of violent confrontations in late 1780. During the earlier pitched battles and threats, the indigenous communities had not dared to profane the church where the creoles, mestizos, several caciques, and their families had taken refuge. Now things changed. In March, during the second week of Lent, a large crowd of Indians led by their new ethnic chiefs besieged the town, just as they had done the previous September and October. This time, however, they had no qualms about penetrating the church. Once inside the building, they carried out a brutal slaughter. According to two Indians involved in the assault, between one hundred and two hundred people were killed; a Spanish official who later investigated the events instead reported 1,037 dead. Women and children of all ages were executed along with the men. The clergy shared the same fate: the parish priest of San Pedro, Isidro Joseph de Herrera, the main authority figure during the earlier clashes, was murdered in the cemetery adjoining the church. At least four other priests died during the attacks. The massacre inside the church building was accompanied by symbolic gestures that underscored the complete rejection of everything the Catholic Church stood for in spiritual and political terms. One of the leaders of the uprising, Pascual Tola, cacique of the Auquimarca community in San Pedro de Buena Vista, recounted that "after having won, they entered the church dancing to flutes and drums, and there they drank until they were drunk and did every wickedness their spite could suggest." The Indians used the sacramental chalices to drink chicha, smashed and profaned the sacred images, made flags and clothes from the priests' vestments, and "while using every lewdness imaginable upon the women, before and after killing them, and while executing this atrocious barbarity, they began to dance carnival jigs over that lake of blood in which the beheaded corpses swam" (Serulnikov 2003: 204–205). Many of the bodies were taken out to the plaza facing the church and were left there unburied as a sign of their diabolical nature.

What months of open revolt had made of colonial power relations is illustrated by the following episode: during the assault on the house of the parish priest, Isidro Joseph de Herrera, the Indians killed a mestiza woman who was just about to give birth; according to a witness, "the baby cried out from the gash they had opened in her belly, and, ripping it out of her body and saying, 'Why should any trace of Cholos remain?' they dashed the baby against the ground" (Serulnikov 2003: 208).

Eventually the attempts to form a unified insurgent movement that could give some sense of coordination to disparate regional uprisings, from Cusco to the southern Andes, proved useless. As mentioned earlier, the alliance between creoles and Indians in Oruro fell apart in a matter of days, and the former abandoned their allegiance to the neo-Inca project altogether. Rumors that Túpac Amaru's troops were marching south turned out to be false. In fact, the Tupamarista army was under assault from royalist forces at that very time. Moreover, insurgent activity in the southern Andes coincided with the arrival of a company of two hundred regular Spanish army soldiers dispatched from Buenos Aires. Under the command of colonel José de Reseguín, the troops arrived in Chichas province a few days after the Indians had executed the corregidor and established the rebel base in the village of Tupiza. Reseguín, a career military officer leading well-trained and well-equipped men, was able to capture the rebel leaders, mobilize the local militias, and regain control of most rural towns across the region. Reseguín entered Chuquisaca on April 19, and over the coming months he would play a central role in the defense of La Paz.

In the end, the defeat of the siege of Chuquisaca began to take its toll on what had been the central core of insurgency in the region: the province of Chayanta. Facing a reinforced royalist army and an offer of pardon for everyone who displayed loyalty to the Crown, many indigenous communities began to reassess their position. Given that the insurrection was carried out by sedentary peasant families and that the battlefields were the places where they and their ancestors had lived for centuries and from which they drew their sustenance, they had neither the inclination nor the ability to flee, so this reconsideration represented their only chance for survival. Political loyalty was a luxury that the Indians of Chayanta, and their peers in other centers of the insurgency, could not afford. It could be said, as historian William B. Taylor has noted in regard to the abruptly conciliatory spirit of Mexican peasants after their frequent revolts in the eighteenth century, that "the villagers had land to farm, families to feed, and a sense of community that was not easily destroyed at one blow" (Taylor 1979: 123).

So the first great rebellion in the Andes ended through an implosion rather than outside military repression. All of the top leaders of the uprisings would be captured and brought before the Audiencia of Charcas by the members of their own communities. All would be publicly executed. The entrance of Spanish troops into the province—an event that had been so often anticipated since the battle of Pocoata in August 1780—took place only after the peasant leaders had already been handed over to the authorities by their peers. By late April, when not a single soldier had yet set foot in Chayanta, the jails of Chuquisaca were so crowded with prisoners that, according to the Audiencia prosecutor, it was impossible to keep up with the legal formalities. Certainly, when confessions were taken, colonial officials realized that many of the Indians who were conducting the felons had been as deeply involved in insurgent activities as the felons themselves. As huge crowds poured into the city to deliver up the guilty, it was not always obvious who was conducting whom. "Having asked [Nicolás] Catari, during his final interrogation, who accompanied him in his looting and atrocious deeds," one witness recalled, "he replied with great integrity: the same ones who had brought him here prisoner" (Serulnikov 2003: 212). But once more, this behavior was only the last line of defense against the harsh realities of war and domination.

Dámaso Katari was executed in the central plaza of Chuquisaca on April 27; his brother Nicolás, on May 7. Ten days later, in the distant city of Cusco, Túpac Amaru would meet the same fate.

11

The Death of Túpac Amaru

The failure of the siege of Cusco marked the beginning of the end for the movement led by Túpac Amaru.[1] The aura surrounding the advent of the new Inca, and the prestige that his early military triumphs gained him, began to vanish after his defeat on the outskirts of the city on January 10, 1781. Perhaps the most ominous impact of the debacle at Picchu had less to do with the human losses and the need to rebuild his forces than with the increasing impossibility of keeping large numbers of the indigenous communities in the region from aligning themselves with the royalist cause. That was crucial, given that the insurgency lacked any significant support among the non-Indian population. It is true that, in the subsequent trial, sixteen creoles and seventeen mestizos would be identified as members of the Tupamarista leadership. But it would be a mistake to take this fact as an indication of the movement's social makeup. The most stable and dependable members of the insurgent command were Túpac Amaru's own relatives: his wife, Micaela Bastidas; his cousin,

1. Historical information and analysis in this section draw on Flores Galindo 2010; O'Phelan Godoy 1985; Walker 1999; Garrett 2003; Stavig 1999; Campbell 1987; Fisher 1966; Lewin 1957; and Serulnikov 2003.

Diego Cristóbal; his nephew, Andrés Mendigure; his son, Mariano Túpac Amaru; and his brother-in-law, Miguel Bastidas. Many of the creoles
implicated in the rebellion were linked to Túpac Amaru by personal
relationships; others might have collaborated occasionally, often under
the pressure of changing circumstances, as the siege of Cusco made
exceedingly clear. At any rate, the creoles and mestizos who did participate were not representatives of large social strata, as was the case in
previous antifiscal urban revolts, in the "Comuneros Revolution" of 1781
in the Colombian Andes, or of course in Oruro. No signs of such a
collective will emerged in Cusco.

The greatest advantages of the Andean armies were their sheer numbers and their adaptation to the terrain. Lacking weaponry or significant
support among Hispanic groups, they could prevail only by virtue of the
massive support of their peers and their skill at taking advantage of the
ravines and gorges of the Peruvian highlands, a landscape they knew
better than anyone. This comparative advantage began to vanish after
their defeat at Picchu: by mid-January, the war in the Cusco region began
to look more and more like a war among Indians. However, those who
joined the side of the Spanish Crown fought alongside well-armed and
organized detachments of the regular army and could count on the
political and economic support of the colonial elites. It is not known
whether they also leaned on the conviction that they were fighting for a
just cause. Nobody ever asked them—for, unlike what happened with
their peers on the other side of the battlefield, the state was never interested in recording their motives or aspirations. All the state cared about
was that they were willing to fight. To be sure, they must have relied on
the belief that they were fighting on the winning side. For peasant communities caught up in a war whose battlefield was their own land, that
was no small matter. The insurgents' ability to mobilize indigenous
forces did not depend exclusively on the perceived justice of their claims;
it also depended on their chances of succeeding. In the Collao and Upper
Peru, the Andean peoples could still continue to forge victorious images
of Túpac Amaru. Not so much in Cusco anymore.

After the defeat at Picchu, the Tupamarista troops split up. Túpac
Amaru's chief collaborator, his cousin Diego Cristóbal Túpac Amaru,
headed north of Cusco to the provinces of Calca, Urubamba, and Paucartambo. He was pursued, however, by a powerful indigenous force under

the royalist cacique Mateo Pumacahua, whose knowledge of the terrain and corresponding fighting tactics equaled the insurgents'. The region north of Cusco, which never embraced the rebellion as vigorously as the southern provinces did, would remain under royalist control. Túpac Amaru, for his part, returned to the Tungasuca area to regroup. There is little information about his activities during the first few months of 1781, but it seems clear that by the time the uprisings in Upper Peru were in full swing—to a large degree because of the very expectations that the figure of Túpac Amaru had awakened—the rebellion in the provinces of Canas y Canchis and Quispicanchis, the primary core of the neo-Inca movement, had stalled.

Late February saw the arrival in Cusco of the Visitor General of the kingdom, José Antonio de Areche—the highest authority in Peru next to the viceroy—and of a well-trained and disciplined force of two hundred soldiers from the regular army battalion of Callao (the port of Lima) under the command of Field Marshal José del Valle. Their objective was to root out the insurrection for good. They began by ratifying the abolition of the forced sale of goods, customs houses, and other such measures that the Cusco authorities had taken after the disaster in Sangarará in order to deactivate the main motives of popular discontent. Moreover, Areche offered a general pardon to any insurgent who switched sides, except for the top leaders and instigators. Persuasion, needless to say, was matched by the use of violence. A few days after arriving in Cusco, Field Marshal del Valle marched south toward Túpac Amaru's fortress in Canas y Canchis. He was at the head of a powerful force of more than seventeen thousand soldiers, the vast majority of them indigenous. The war in Cusco, again, was to a large extent a war among Indians.

On learning that a magistrate of the rank and influence of Visitor General Areche had arrived in Cusco, Túpac Amaru sent him a long letter from his encampment in Tinta. This text, dated March 5, 1781, just two weeks before the royalist army reached the insurgent base, is perhaps the last comprehensive testimony of his thinking. It takes the form of a list of grievances. Let us listen to his voice.

Atheists, Calvinists, and Lutherans: The main cause of poverty among the Indians was the reparto system. "This accursed and corrupt reparto," he said, "has placed us in this most deplorable state of death through its enormous excess." In a tacit justification of the execution of Antonio de

Arriaga, he noted that the corregidor's own bookkeeping records, which were now in his hands, showed that he had collected more than 300,000 pesos from the reparto, though the legal limit was 112,000 pesos. Among the goods distributed, there were needles, blue powders, playing cards, and "other sorts of ridiculous trinkets like these." Payments were collected through all manner of extortions. But Arriaga hadn't been the exception; all corregidores were like him, more infamous than the "Attilas and Neros" of this world, for at least those tyrants "had some excuse, for after all they were infidels; whereas the corregidores, though baptized, prove themselves unworthy of Christianity through their works, and instead seem Atheists, Calvinists, and Lutherans, for they are enemies of God and of men, idolaters of gold and silver" (Lewin 1957: 474–475).

Worse than slaves: The heavy debts that the Indians contracted forced them to work for poverty wages on the large private landholdings. The hacienda owners, "looking upon us as worse than slaves, make us work from two in the morning until the stars appear after nightfall, with no more wages than two reales a day: besides this, they burden us on Sundays with chores" (Lewin 1957: 476).

Vomiting blood: As to forced labor in Potosí and Huancavelica (the largest mercury mine in the Americas, where workers were in constant contact with the deadly metal), Túpac Amaru argued that mita Indians had to "walk for more than three months" to reach the mines, yet they received no pay for the journey. The tribunals spurned his cries for the abolition of this dreadful burden, the direct consequence of which was nothing less than "to destroy the kingdom and its towns by killing its Indians, who scarcely return to their villages when, within a month or so, they depart this life, vomiting blood" (Lewin 1957: 476–477).

Tapestries and tatters: Parish priests were no better. The Indians were forced to offer them enormous ecclesiastical fees and *ricuchicus*—large baskets of agricultural products—in return for celebrating their religious fiestas, but they used this wealth only for "the pomp, splendor, and vanity of their own families," not for the welfare of their parishes. The priests were rich; the churches where their indigenous parishioners prayed were destitute. "In their parish parsonages . . . one sees the best tapestries, mirrors, fixtures of marquetry; and in the church buildings, rags and tatters." Due to the priests' greed, their indifference toward their pastoral duties, and their ignorance of the "language of this land," their Indian parishioners reached adulthood not knowing even how to cross themselves (Lewin 1957: 480).

Compassionate heart: Why had they decided to rise up against this state of affairs? Because they could never get their complaints heard before the Royal Council. This was surely not the king's fault; "the reason must be that [these complaints] had never reached the royal ears; for it is impossible that such crying, wailing, and hardships among his poor and wretched provincial subjects from every rank should fail to move the compassionate heart and noble breast of the King my Lord" (Lewin 1957: 474).

In his response, José Antonio de Areche, one of the chief architects of the new Bourbon imperial policies, a man accustomed to reflecting on Spanish imperial rule from a global perspective, went straight to the heart of the matter. Who was he, Túpac Amaru, to undermine the loyalty to the king of "the subjects whom the heavens bestow on Him?" Túpac Amaru appeared not to understand the enormity of his crimes; "the chains that you are dragging," Areche told him, did not seem to be weighing him down yet, but "they very soon will," he added (Lewin 1957: 481). Many of the grievances he listed ("the afflictions that the provinces suffered because of [repartos]," the mita system, the lack of pay in textile workshops and on haciendas, or "the coldness with which religion has been administered to them") were in the process of being resolved, or measures had already been taken to relieve them (Lewin 1957: 483). If this were the true motive behind the rebellion, he wondered, wouldn't it have been more sensible—instead of luring thousands of Indians to their downfall and "perhaps to their eternal damnation"—to "bear with the old ills a bit longer, intercede with God for remedy, and inform the high authorities of the Nation in order to redress them"? (Lewin 1957: 483). Certainly it did. But Areche knew all too well that these were not the true motives behind the rebellion. "You, sir," he recalled, "have pretended to have actual orders to kill corregidores without a hearing or due process simply to relieve the Indians of every burden, even the just ones" (Lewin 1957: 482). In his letter, Túpac Amaru had denied that his aim had been "to refuse allegiance to our monarch, to crown myself king, to return to idolatry" (Lewin 1957: 478). But the incriminating evidence against him was overwhelming. "You, sir," Areche reminded him, "have issued a proclamation on the death of the Europeans, and you have displayed in all kinds of documents clauses filled with horror and injustice, inhumanity and irreligion; and yet despite all this you pretend not to be taken as a blasphemer, as an apostate, and as a rebel" (Lewin 1957: 482). He advised Túpac Amaru not to wait until he was captured but to prostrate himself voluntarily before "the feet of justice" (Lewin 1957: 484); not to expect clemency, but to accept with resignation the punishment for his affronts to God, the king, and the world in general, "for all that you have done to scandalize it," and to which he was going to bequeath a "sad memory for many centuries to come" (Lewin 1957: 485).

In his letter, dated Cusco, March 12, Areche warned Túpac Amaru that he would soon be facing "a large and well-armed army" (Lewin 1957: 484). Indeed, within a few days Field Marshal José del Valle led the army into its first encounter against insurgent forces in the province of Cotabambas. The indigenous troops were defeated, and their leaders, Túpac Amaru's two main creole lieutenants, Tomás Parvina and Felipe Miguel Bermúdez, died in combat. Then the royal army marched on Canas y Canchis to confront Túpac Amaru's own forces, composed at that time of some seven thousand men. Realizing his big military disadvantage, the Inca tried to organize a surprise attack before the regular army could reach him, but a deserter warned del Valle in advance, and the maneuver had to be aborted. On March 23, six columns of royalist soldiers encamped on the outskirts of Tinta, some two leagues from the main insurgent base. The rebel troops were surrounded. Since their positions were difficult to reach, del Valle was patient: he decided on laying siege to them until the lack of provisions forced them to surrender. So it was that, on April 5, when food had indeed run out, Túpac Amaru made a desperate attempt at breaking the blockade, but his forces were defeated. Túpac Amaru himself sought to escape by swimming across a river and hiding in the nearby town of Langui. But the next day, betrayed by some of his own followers, he was captured by a group of soldiers from Lima and handed over to del Valle.

Túpac Amaru, his wife Micaela Bastidas, two of their sons, and a few other insurgent leaders were conducted to the pueblo of Urcos, Quispicanchis province, about eight leagues from Cusco. Areche was waiting for them there. On April 14, the Visitor General entered the imperial city with his famous prisoner. According to one contemporary account, "Don José Gabriel Túpac Amaru traveled sitting like a woman on a sidesaddle, with shackles on his feet, his head uncovered so that everyone might see him . . . wearing on his chest, dangling from a chain, a Golden Cross with its Holy Christ; he was dressed in socks of white silk and shoes of black velvet; his serene countenance and color characteristic of the Inca." Behind the "wretched Inca" came his wife "on a white mule, sitting without a sidesaddle, without a hat, so that she might be recognized" (Lewin 1957: 491). Everyone in the city turned out into the streets to watch the procession go by.

Túpac Amaru was housed in a former Jesuit monastery that had been converted into a barracks. He was interrogated and subjected to torture for several weeks to make him confess the names of his creole allies, how he had organized the uprising, and what their future plans were. His death sentence was carried out on May 18. The night before, on Areche's orders, the bishop of Cusco exhorted Túpac Amaru and his associates "not to take leave of the world without first declaring completely all their accomplices in the rebellion, for otherwise they would leave behind a perpetual ferment, making them responsible for it before God and deserving of eternal punishment" (Lewin 1957: 496). But the Inca appeared to regret nothing, and as far as we know, he said nothing. According to some reports, in answer to the adamant requests of Areche to yield up the names of his accomplices, Túpac Amaru replied, "Here there are no accomplices besides you and me: you for oppressing the people, and me for trying to free them." It is uncertain whether the quote is authentic or apocryphal. His political testament, in any case, was discovered in one of his pockets when he was captured. It is a coronation edict, signed by "Don José I, by the Grace of God, Inca, King of Peru, Santa Fe [de Bogotá], Quito, Chile, Buenos Aires, and the Continent of the Southern Seas," which reads as follows:

> The kings of Castile have been usurping the Crown and dominions of my people for nearly three centuries, burdening my subjects with intolerable taxes and tribute payments, excises, military payments, customs duties, alcabalas, monopolies, contracts, tithes, royal fifths, viceroys, Audiencias, corregidores and other ministers, *all equal in their tyranny.* (Lewin 1957: 427, emphasis added)

The following morning he, his wife, one of their sons, his uncle, and others in his circle were conducted to the city's central plaza. Túpac Amaru was obliged to witness how the executioners hanged all his relatives after cutting out their tongues. Micaela Bastidas was sentenced to be throttled by the cruel garrote, but since her neck was too slender for the device to strangle her, "it was necessary for the executioners, tying ropes around her neck, pulling in both directions, and bracing their feet against her stomach and chest, to finish killing her" (Lewin 1957: 497). Túpac Amaru was then freed from all his shackles and chains, his tongue was cut out, and ropes were tied to his four extremities, which were then tied to the saddle straps of four horses so that they would quarter his body. Nothing like it had ever been seen in Cusco. The horses were not strong enough to quarter his body, though they pulled hard on it for a long time. The grotesque cruelty of this martyrdom made Areche decide to halt the execution. Túpac Amaru was then untied, carried to the scaffold, and beheaded. Afterward his arms and legs were cut off.

One eyewitness of these events recalled that the crowd that thronged the plaza stood mute before the brutal spectacle. The audience, moreover, included no one of indigenous origin, or at least no one wearing traditional Indian attire. Around midday, while the horses were still tugging fruitlessly at the body, a strong wind picked up, followed immediately by an intense rain shower. One contemporary account stated, "This is the reason the Indians have taken to saying that heaven and the elements mourned the death of the Inca, whom the inhuman and impious Spaniards were killing with such cruelty" (Lewin 1957: 498).

The bodies of Túpac Amaru and his wife were taken a few days later to Picchu, the hill where the insurgent army had encamped during their siege of the imperial city. They were left exposed there for a while, then finally burned in a bonfire. The Inca's limbs were likewise put on display: his arms in Tungasuca and in the capital of Carabaya province, his legs in the villages of Livitaca (Chumbivilcas province) and Santa Rosa (Lampa province). This exhibition of his body fragments was followed by a less bloody but politically no less significant ritual—a sign of the times to come. Colonial officials were ordered to gather up all the records of Túpac Amaru's family tree that had been filed in the archives of the Audiencia of Lima, the court where the Cusco leader had spent years litigating for the recognition of his Inca lineage. Once they were collected, they were to be publicly burned in the central plaza of Lima "so that no memory of such documents might remain" (Lewin 1957: 496).

12

....

The Heirs

The capture and execution of Túpac Amaru did not put a stop to the rebellion in Peru, but it did force a change in its leadership, geographical core, and combat tactics.[1] The Inca's martyrdom actually ended up radicalizing the violence. Command of the insurgency was passed down to José Gabriel's relatives: his cousin, Diego Cristóbal Túpac Amaru, who had been involved in the rebellion since the capture of corregidor Arriaga; his nephew Andrés Mendigure; his son, Mariano; and his brother-in-law, Miguel Bastidas. All were very young. Diego Cristóbal, the new head of the movement, was scarcely twenty-six years old; Mariano was eighteen; and Andrés, the most daring and active of the Tupamarista officers, just seventeen. But their youth should not mislead us. In a society where life expectancy was only about forty, their ages had a very different meaning than they would in modern times. Moreover, months of uninterrupted war had given them invaluable experience. They knew what they were doing. And the first thing they did, compelled in part by

1. Historical information and analysis in this section draw on Flores Galindo 2010; O'Phelan Godoy 1985; Walker 1999; Garrett 2003; Stavig 1999; Campbell 1987; Fisher 1966; Lewin 1957; and Serulnikov 2003.

circumstances, was to move the center of the rebellion south to the provinces around Lake Titicaca. This region, the Collao, had proved to be one of the bastions of the insurgency during the campaign led by Túpac Amaru in late 1780, and unlike in the Cusco region, indigenous communities here had joined the uprising without regard to their caciques' choices. I have already discussed how the peasants in Azángaro, the new capital of the revolution, had not hesitated to rise up against the Choqueguanca family, one of the most prosperous noble Inca families anywhere in the Andes. Having aligned with the royalist cause, the Choqueguancas had to flee to save their lives. In the Collao provinces of Lampa, Azángaro, Puno, and Chucuito, the Spanish regular army found itself in enemy territory, surrounded by an indifferent or hostile indigenous population from which they could expect little or nothing: no reinforcements, no provisions, no information. In the southern highlands, the campaign against the insurgents, which seemed to have so much momentum after the victory in Cusco, suddenly came to a standstill.

The war took on new traits during this period. In the provinces of the Collao, the insurgent forces fully embraced guerrilla tactics. Commander del Valle's army, which had marched south to pacify the region only hours after transferring the custody of Túpac Amaru to Areche, found itself under constant assault by small insurgent groups. They would ambush the soldiers, mount surprise attacks, and then retreat. The royalist troops got a foretaste of what lay ahead near Langui, the same town where Túpac Amaru had been captured a few weeks earlier. On April 18 and April 20, a nightly assault by forces under the command of Diego Cristóbal inflicted so many casualties on the colonial army that del Valle had to suspend the march for several days while reinforcements were drummed up. At the same time, del Valle found himself obliged to rely more and more on his own troops, for the indigenous communities of Anta, Chinchero, and other Cusco areas that had proved so helpful during the campaigns in Tinta now refused to follow him. Instead of walking south into the Collao, they returned home. As the royalists marched through the provinces of Azángaro, Lampa, and Carabaya, they met with deserted villages devoid of cattle, grain, and provisions. They also met with an enemy determined to win the war at any cost. The insurgents seemed to understand that hostile Indians posed as great a danger to their survival as the royalist army did. And they acted on that understanding. For example, they started to cut off the noses, ears, or arms of any who served as a messengers for the army, as a warning to the rest. As one might expect, no Indian wanted to expose himself to such horrors, no matter how much money the royalists offered. All the women in the town of Icho, Puno province, were decapitated because their husbands were considered royalists. In Quesque, the indigenous forces attacked an army column with great ferocity; in the course of battle they shouted that they weren't cowards like the men of Tinta and that the soldiers would see what awaited them. In April, the town of Paucarcolla, capital of the province of the same name, was set ablaze.

Faced with a fierce enemy and the open or concealed hostility of the local populace, the army did what so many other armies, in different times and places, have done under similar circumstances: it unleashed a more or less indiscriminate campaign of terror. A case in point is the cold-blooded execution of one-fifth of the men in the village of Santa Rosa just because they were suspected of collaborating with the enemy. After the execution of the Inca, there was no room for neutrality—at least not in the provinces of the Collao. But it was the Spanish army, not the Tupamarista forces, that suffered the most from isolation. The topography of the region and the arrival of winter did not help them much, either. Most of the soldiers had come from Lima and other lowland regions in Peru. Their ability to adapt to the demands of a prolonged war against an elusive enemy at altitudes of more than 3,500 meters proved slim. As the troops found themselves at odds with the local people, short of supplies, and lashed by the cold, their morale plummeted.

The battle for the control of southern Peru was centered on the city of Puno. Located on the northern shore of Lake Titicaca, at some 3,800 meters above sea level, near the silver mines of Cancharani and Lyacayata, Puno soon became the chief royalist bastion in the region. The city had already undergone massive incursions during Túpac Amaru's campaign in the Collao in late 1780. The corregidor of Puno province, Joaquín Antonio de Orellana, had in fact been forced to flee; he was only able to return in early 1781, after the war had focused once more on Cusco. Then, when the core of insurgent activity returned south, Puno came under fiercer attack than ever, this time at the hands of the Inca's successors. These assaults took place in a context of a generalized upheaval not only in southern Peru but also in the entire region surrounding Lake Titicaca. By March 1781 the La Paz region, on the other side of the lake, had finally risen up. The Upper Peruvian provinces of Sicasica, Pacajes, Omasuyos, and Larecaja were almost entirely under the control of their indigenous communities. In March, corregidor Orellana dispatched some of the Puno militia companies to several places on the western shore of Lake Titicaca, but he could not prevent towns such as Juli, Ilabe, and Chucuito from being occupied and looted by the Indians. Only the Lupacas, a group whose ethnic tensions with other communities of the Collao had very deep historical roots, remained loyal to the Crown. Facing an imminent attack on the city, Orellana requested urgent reinforcements. Commander del Valle's army was in no condition to help, however; the royalist forces of Upper Peru, even less so. The city was on its own.

The first assault on Puno took place on March 10, when eighteen thousand men under the command of Diego Cristóbal appeared in the surrounding mountains. At that time the city could count on a force of around four thousand soldiers, plus a hundred or so royalist Indians. The insurgents reached as far as the outskirts of Puno, and some of their shots even landed in the main plaza. The city militias were nevertheless able to hold on, and Diego Cristóbal ordered a tactical retreat. But not for long. That April and May, indigenous communities from the provinces of Azángaro, Lampa, and Carabaya would besiege Puno at least three more times. The most violent of these assaults took place on May 7, when the forces of Diego Cristóbal and the Indians from the neighboring town of Chucuito managed to isolate the city completely. Lake Titicaca became its only means of communication with the outside world. There were gory battles that lasted many days. Diego Cristóbal, reluctant to risk everything on a single battle, decided to withdraw once more and regroup while waiting for a better opportunity. The Chucuito Indians, however, continued with their attacks for several more days. The fall of Puno seemed just a matter of time.

Fearing that disaster was looming, Commander del Valle finally gave in to corregidor Orellana's exhortations and marched to Puno with his decimated troops. He arrived on May 24. The indigenous forces then withdrew to the nearby mountains. From there they watched the regular army's maneuvers. A few hours later, following a pattern that by then was familiar, they dispersed instead of exposing themselves to multiple casualties. Orellana thought that the time had at last arrived to pursue and exterminate the rebel forces, to root out that evil once and for all. He did not know that the worst was yet to come.

The army that arrived in Puno was a shadow of the powerful force that had defeated Túpac Amaru. Of the seventeen thousand men who had begun the march from Cusco to the Collao, hardly more than a thousand soldiers and about 450 loyalist Indians remained. The lack of pay, the scarcity of food, the harshness of winter, and their powerlessness in the face of the Indians tactics all led to the desertion en masse of the soldiers from Lima, Cochabamba, and other places. Most of the Indians, for their part, had returned to their hometowns or had gone over to the rebel side. Del Valle had serious doubts about whether the troops stationed in Puno could stand up to a mass attack. A council of war was then held, at which it was decided that the army should withdraw to Cusco rather than run the risk of being exterminated by the enemy or decimated by desertions. Del Valle offered to leave Orellana a guard of hundred soldiers, but this force was manifestly inadequate. The corregidor could not even guarantee that he would be able to feed them.

A decision was thus made to evacuate Puno. The inhabitants were given three days to prepare. On May 26, some five thousand men, women, and children took whatever they could carry and began the exodus. The city was left empty and at the mercy of the insurgents. The tactic of successive assaults and withdrawals had at last borne fruit. The Puno neighbors set off on a march to Cusco, corregidor Orellana leading the way. Along the road they were repeatedly harassed by rebel squads. Casualties mounted as the days went by. To make matters worse, the high colonial magistrates disagreed on the next course of action. The viceroy of Peru, Agustín de Jáuregui, and Visitor General Antonio de Areche reproved Commander del Valle's decision to abandon Puno and instructed Orellana to return immediately. As the Puno dwellers were already nearing Cusco, and the request was probably unrealizable anyway, the order was ignored. On June 5, after some forty days of marching and countless hardships, Orellana and his people arrived in the imperial city. It took a few more days for del Valle to reach Cusco, because he had decided to head first to Carabaya province and make contact there with a detachment of some eight hundred soldiers who had been left isolated due to the lack of messengers. Desertions were so rampant by then that for a time the commander feared he might be completely abandoned by his soldiers.

In June 1781, the predicament of the royalist forces in the southern Peruvian highlands could not have been more somber. Del Valle's once powerful army had practically disbanded. The refugees from Puno were ordered to return to their city, but the corregidor refused to do so without the backing of a force of at least four thousand well-trained soldiers. His repeated requests to the other corregidores in the region to send him military aid fell on deaf ears. The Collao was, for all practical purposes, in the hands of the insurgents. Even near Cusco, rebel indigenous groups from the provinces of Calca, Paucartambo, and Canas y Canchis resumed the attacks. Not even Cusco seemed completely safe anymore. The top military leaders in the region, Areche and del Valle, began a feud over counterinsurgency policies that would drag on for years. Areche condemned the military disaster in the Collao and recommended doubling the forces there in order to annihilate the insurgents. Del Valle believed that escalating the conflict was unfeasible and suicidal. In a letter addressed to the viceroy of Peru in early August, he advocated for granting a general amnesty to all the rebels, beginning with the Amarus themselves. The Collao campaign had taught him that negotiation, not war, was the only way to pacify the kingdom.

Meanwhile, Diego Cristóbal had managed to establish an Inca court of sorts in the town of Azángaro. There he received daily visits from people coming from various provinces, planned the next moves along with Andrés Túpac Amaru, Miguel Bastidas, and other rebel leaders, and gathered silver and valuables captured in combat. Every night he attended mass in the village church, a very old building whose walls "were covered with paintings by great masters in rich golden frames, and the main altar was covered over with solid silver plates." He behaved, and was seen by his followers, as an Inca. The death of Túpac Amaru had not changed things very much after all.

What actually would change the course of the rebellion, and ultimately seal its fate, was what was happening at that time on the other side of Lake Titicaca. In this respect, Areche's order for Orellana and del Valle to return to Puno and regain command over the city may have been impracticable, but it was not capricious. Retaking Puno was a crucial step in providing military support to the colonial armies that had been fighting for weeks over the control of the city of La Paz and the surrounding region. And the fate of the Andean insurgency would ultimately revolve around the outcome of that battle.

13

"Tomás Túpac-Katari, Inca King"

Over the course of the eighteenth century, La Paz grew into one of the most vibrant commercial hubs in the Andes.[1] It was an important coca-producing area at a time when coca was a mass consumer good in all the urban centers of Peru and Upper Peru. By the 1780s, La Paz had a population of forty thousand, making it the fastest-growing city in the region. Merchants and hacienda owners dominated the local political scene. On March 13, 1781, around the time the royalist armies were encircling the Tupamarista forces in Tinta, the inhabitants of La Paz woke up to the news that some forty thousand Indian men and women had occupied the high plain known as El Alto overlooking their city. They intended to attack.

Whereas the insurgent army did aim to seize the city by force, the strategy was not to do it by outright assault. Instead the rebels planned to control El Alto, undertake surprise raids, cut off the few access routes into the city, and wait for its hunger-stricken inhabitants to lose their will to resist and to surrender. No other city in the Andes, possibly no other

1. Historical information and analysis in this section draw on Thomson 2002. Very useful material was also found in Valle de Siles 1990; Fisher 1966; and Lewin 1957.

city in the Americas, presented such favorable physical conditions for this type of war of attrition. La Paz is built at the bottom of a deep depression, a veritable gorge. An enemy force can disrupt its communications with the outside world relatively easily by occupying the pampa or high plateau that nearly encircles it. The Indian encampment in El Alto on March 13 set in motion an unprecedented siege that would last 109 consecutive days. By the time it was finally lifted, around ten thousand residents had lost their lives. There never had been, nor would there ever again be, a more devastating indigenous attack on the Spanish population in the Andes.

In the early days of the siege, the people of La Paz learned for the first time about a man who would become the most prominent emblem of the insurgency in Upper Peru: Túpac Katari. In fact, few if any references to him appear in accounts of the earlier clashes that had convulsed the La Paz highland rural towns. Unlike Túpac Amaru and Tomás Katari, whose political trajectories can be traced back several years before the events of 1780, Túpac Katari burst in upon the historical record together with the siege of La Paz. With this episode alone his name would come to be associated, as if the extraordinary magnitude of the event absorbed all the luminosity of his character. His real name was Julián Apaza. He had been born some thirty years earlier near the town of Sicasica. Later on he established himself as a tribute-paying outsider (*forastero*) in an ayllu of the Ayoayo community, Sicasica province. He was an Aymara speaker, like all Indians in that area. He described himself as small trader of coca and locally produced cloth—in other words, one of the many indigenous petty merchants who connected the lowland coca-producing valleys to Potosí, Chuquisaca, Oruro, Cusco, and other Andean urban centers. It was around these trade activities—often carried out by traveling indigenous merchants or *trajinantes*, as the Julián Apazas of this world were then called—that the regional economy of La Paz had flourished during the previous decades. Not much can be said of the ideology and mental outlook of someone about whom so little is known. It is plausible to imagine that he was accustomed to a harsh life on the road, to dealing with people of diverse social and ethnic backgrounds, to having to win the respect of others, and to defending what he believed to be his own, by force if necessary. He must have forged an overall view of society somewhat different—wider and less hierarchical, perhaps—from peasants such as Tomás Katari, who were more tied to the land (although no Andean peasants were entirely devoted to farming). In the resting places along the roads and the urban markets people met with strangers (mule drivers, petty traders, mestizo shopkeepers, and the like) and exchanged news about what was going on in different parts of the country.

In a matter of weeks, Túpac Katari would achieve a power and prominence comparable only to that of Túpac Amaru himself. But he was a very different type of leader. Hardly a prosperous, educated cacique accustomed to breaking bread with the colonial elites, he did not speak fluent Spanish, belonged to no noble lineage, and had never held an important office in his community before the rebellion. Túpac Amaru, with his Inca ancestry, his wealth, and his cultivated manners, projected an aura of authority. Túpac Katari had to win people's allegiance; he couldn't take it for granted. According to Fray Matías Borda, a cleric who was forced to celebrate mass for the indigenous forces at El Alto and witnessed first-hand what happened in the insurgent camp, "there were many who disputed the government of this Katari. They said, if an Indian with minimum family obligations, the son of an unknown father—and at best the illegitimate son of so-and-so Apaza sexton, an occupation he trained in—as well as being by nature very rude, since he didn't even know how to read . . . if he had himself Crowned or made chief, why shouldn't they do same, given that they were *principales* and legitimately worthy of respect?" (quoted in Thomson 2002: 190–191). His general attitude toward the dominant culture was also very different from that of his counterpart in Cusco. Borda himself recalled that when he was introduced to Túpac Katari, "I greeted him in Spanish, and he reproved me, commanding me to speak no language other than Aymara, which Law he had imposed under pain of death" (Lewin 1957: 528).

The siege of La Paz caught the authorities by surprise. But the attack was the corollary of short- and long-term political experiences. Much like what happened in the Charcas region to the south, the crisis of the colonial order in the region of La Paz (Omasuyos, Larecaja, Sicasica, Pacajes, and Chucuito provinces) had begun to take shape much earlier, as far back as the 1740s, with the expansion of the forced sale of goods and the corregidores' increasingly discretionary removal and appointment of community chiefs. In fact, the highland communities of La Paz showed an unmatched record of collective mobilization in the whole

Andean region. Such was the case of the mass uprisings in the town of Chuani (Larecaja province) in the late 1740s, Sicasica in 1769, Chulumani (a lowland pueblo in Sicasica province) in 1771, and Caquiavari (Pacajes province), also in 1771. I have already mentioned the uproar unleashed by the execution of the corregidores of the provinces of Paria and Carangas. Now, in the early 1770s, two corregidores had already been killed by the Indians in Pacajes and Sicasica provinces.

Recent studies have shown that these social movements were not mere reactions to abuses by corregidores and caciques or to the steady decline in the living conditions of the Andean peoples since the mid-eighteenth century. They also stemmed from profound transformations in the social structure and authority system of the Aymara communities. Since the Spanish conquest, the groups that had constituted the ancient Aymara chiefdoms of the Collao had been abandoning their former practice of occupying agricultural plots in a variety of dispersed ecological zones and had been gravitating instead toward nucleated communities with contiguous land areas. Unlike the ethnic groups of northern Potosí, whose component ayllus displayed a high level of symbolic and economic integration, communities here remained grouped into what have been defined as "confederations of ayllus" headed by regional hereditary caciques (Klein 1993: 58–60). Some of these caciques, such as the Fernández Guarachi family in the pueblo of Jesús de Machaca (Pacajes province), came to amass sizable fortunes. These confederations fell into crisis after the mid-eighteenth century as local ayllus began to contest their subordination to the noble Andean lords of the larger social groupings. The newly emerging community-level authorities were traditional local ayllu leaders—tribute collectors, or *jilacatas*, and elected elders. Power was thus beginning to be transferred from the top of the community to the base, in a progressive democratization of authority systems that undermined traditional aristocratic principles.

Moreover, the recurring revolts against rural overlords gave rise to wider symbolic challenges to colonial power relationships. These challenges were mostly unrelated to outright rejections of Crown sovereignty, notions of Inca restoration, or millenarian expectations—the ideological representations usually associated with Andean anticolonial protest movements. Instead sedition appeared through a set of political practices that undermined the very foundations of colonial society. These "peasant visions of Andean utopia," as the historian Sinclair Thomson has defined them, included the physical elimination of the agents of Spanish domination; the search for greater regional indigenous autonomy, even if under nominal subjection to the Crown; and the subordination of the non-Indian population to Andean political and cultural hegemony (Thomson 2002: 162). For example, in 1771 the Aymara communities adopted a practice that would become very common a decade later during the general Tupamarista uprising: they forced all the mestizo and creole townspeople of Caquiaviri, capital of Pacajes province, to take an oath of "obedience to them and to wear Indian mantles, tunics, and headgear, and their women had to wear acsu [the wrapped dress of Andean women] just as they do, and in this way they would go free and keep their lives" (Thomson 2002: 157–158). Though bounded in space and time, these movements were not sudden, spontaneous eruptions of violence, but the results of prolonged and complex political conflicts. Nor were they the initiatives of a few ringleaders. The course of actions tended, rather, to be set by community assemblies and collective deliberations. It was in the community, the común, that decision-making power lay. As was proclaimed after the corregidor of Pacajes was executed in 1771, "Now that the corregidor was dead, there was no other magistrate for them; instead, the king was the community for whom they ruled" (Thomson 2002: 151).

This long-standing experience of contention and the egalitarian ideas shaping Indian local protest help to explain the distinctive meaning La Paz peasants attributed to the pan-Andean upheaval. There were no illusions about cross-racial alliances against imperial policies, as in Cusco, or about the reenactment of an ideal ayllu-state reciprocity pact against rural overlords, as in northern Potosí. From the outset, the movement here assumed unmistakably anticolonial overtones. Furthermore, the La Paz uprising, in great measure due to its timing and geographical location, could be simultaneously nurtured by the egalitarian drive of the indigenous movement in Charcas and the neo-Inca aspirations of the Andean people in Cusco. Túpac Katari himself, while traveling around the region in February, said he had been commissioned by Túpac Amaru to rouse and organize the Aymara communities. He displayed edicts from the Inca and spelled out his relationship to the new king by proclaiming himself "viceroy." A few weeks before the siege of La Paz began, for example, he demanded the allegiance of the indigenous authorities of Sicasica province, arguing, "I am the one who rules as viceroy, a position to which I have been elevated by His Excellence the Inca" (Valle de Siles 1990: 37).

The influences from the south were no less significant. The highland peoples of La Paz kept very close tabs on the events in the Charcas region, particularly the disturbances in Oruro. In March and April of 1781, as the three successive indigenous assaults on the mining town unfolded, several communities in Sicasica, the heart of the Katarista rebellion, were in contact with communities in Oruro and Paria provinces. Coordinating the participation of the Sicasica Indians in the assaults on Oruro was the aforementioned Santos Mamani from the Challapata community, the most radical leader in the region. The Aymara communities seemed to draw a lesson from this experience: it was futile to expect creoles to join their political project. The enemy was increasingly identified by the Aymara word q'ara, which means anyone who is not Indian. Q'ara was not a strictly racial category; it could designate mestizos or whites, but also everyone who did not dress like an Indian, or simply anyone who opposed the rebellion, regardless of ethnic origin. It did have distinctive socioeconomic overtones. Santos Mamani, for example, declared that "the time had come for the relief of Indians and the annihilation of Spaniards and creoles whom they called 'q'aras,' which in their language means 'naked,' because without paying taxes or laboring they were the owners of what they [the Indians] worked on, under the yoke and burdened with many obligations. They obtained the benefits, while the Indians spent their lives oppressed, knocked about, and in utter misfortune" (quoted in Thomson 2002: 216).

These two currents thus converged in the La Paz highlands. This confluence was perfectly symbolized by the name that Julián Apaza adopted. On occasion, his followers even referred to him as "Tomás Túpac-Katari." He, in turn, came to present himself with a more explicit title still: "Tomás Túpac-Katari, Inca king" (Thomson 2002: 189).

14

War against the Q'aras

The aftershocks of the Cusco upheaval were late to come to the La Paz region.[1] The first alarm bells went off in December 1780, during the campaign of the Tupamarista army through the Collao provinces, especially Azángaro, Lampa, and Paucarcolla. The massive assaults on rural towns and haciendas led the corregidores of Sicasica, Omasuyos, Pacajes, and Larecaja provinces to try establishing a military cordon to prevent Cusco's insurgent forces from expanding their operations into Upper Peru. For the time being, their fears proved unfounded. Let's insist once more: no social movement in colonial America ever spread as widely as the Tupamarista movement did, but it was not the revolutionaries that traveled well; it was the revolution. Thus, in February 1781, while Túpac Amaru's forces were absorbed in the war against the royal armies in Cusco, many indigenous groups in Sicasica, Yungas, and Pacajes began to rise up in the name of Túpac Amaru against landowners, merchants, colonial officials, and townspeople. All the creoles and mestizos were forced to leave rural areas and seek refuge, with their goods and cattle, in

1. Historical information and analysis in this section draw on Thomson 2002. The section is also based on Valle de Siles 1990; Fisher 1966; and Lewin 1957.

just a few villages. Sorata, capital of Larecaja province, was the main one. The pan-Andean revolution was long in reaching La Paz, but when it arrived it hit in full fury.

In view of the magnitude of the upheaval, the military commander in La Paz, Sebastián de Segurola, decided to lead a punitive expedition into the zone. Segurola had been the corregidor of Larecaja until December 1780, when, because of the widespread state of unrest, he was made head of the regional military forces. In February he sent two columns of some six hundred men to Viacha (Pacajes province) and Laja (Omasuyos province). The army immediately found ominous signs: in contrast to the Cusco region, here it was impossible to recruit Indians to the royalist cause. Recall that even in Canas y Canchis, the core of the Tupamarista movement, some communities had aligned with the colonial authorities. In the La Paz region, scarcely more than a handful approached the army—and their true intentions were rather dubious. Segurola ordered all suspects of sedition, pretty much everybody, ruthlessly repressed. According to testimony by the royalist soldiers themselves, some three hundred Indians were put to the sword in Viacha. In Laja, as the Indians had fled before the troops arrived, every house in the town was set on fire. Some of the Indians sought refuge on a nearby hill. Although there were only a few dozen individuals, they put up such fierce resistance that the column commanded by Segurola had to request reinforcements. Another ominous sign: for the insurgents, this was a fight to the death. The commander reflected that his enemies had "a spirit and a determination so horrible that they could serve as an example to the bravest nation" (Valle de Siles 1990: 171). Little surprise, then, that the colonial army's campaign of terror, far from terrifying the indigenous peoples, provoked an equal and opposite force: a massive march on the city of La Paz. The beginning of the siege found Segurola still in the field.

The Tupamarista revolution in the La Paz highlands was therefore not, as colonial authorities had feared, the result of the southward expansion of insurgent armies from Cusco: it was a rebellion of local populations in the name of Túpac Amaru. And the allusion to Túpac Amaru's edicts and proclamations was much more symbolic than instrumental. While the Inca strove, albeit with little success, to build cross-racial and cross-class coalitions, the Aymara rebel forces were inspired by overt nativist notions. An episode that occurred early in the rebellion made clear the meaning Túpac Amaru had taken on in this regional context. In front of a large crowd of Indians who had gathered in the outskirts of the small village of Tiquina, near Copacabana in Omasuyos province, an emissary of Túpac Katari proclaimed that the Inca king ordered them to execute all corregidores, caciques, tax collectors, and "any person who is or appears to be a Spaniard," not excepting women or children, or, if it came to that, priests (Thomson 2002: 212). The rebels proceeded to assault the church where all the townspeople had gathered and kill them one by one, the men killing men, the women killing women. Despite the priest's pleas, they would not allow the hundred or so bodies to be buried. They said that the Inca sovereign had ordered them to leave them exposed to the weather so that the dogs and scavenger birds would eat them; the town dwellers were, after all, nothing but demons and the accursed. In itself the incident was not much different from what was happening in various rural villages in Chayanta or Cochabamba, such as the aforementioned attacks on San Pedro de Buena Vista and Tapacarí. What set it apart is that here it formed part of an articulated political movement that had a clear structure of leadership and was determined to take power and seize control of the kingdom. They had a king for a reason, and a viceroy, too.

The events in Tiquina took place on March 19, 1781. Only six days earlier, insurgent forces had encamped outside La Paz. They were not going to stay there only for a few days, as other insurgents had done in Cusco, Chuquisaca, and Oruro. They would remain there as long as necessary, as long as they could hold on. It would not be long enough to achieve their goal. But it would be long enough to provoke the largest massacre of q'aras the Andean world had witnessed since the sixteenth century, since the distant times when the armies of the Pizarros and Almagros had conquered their ancestors in the name of a king and a god they had never heard of.

15

The Battle for La Paz

The indigenous forces converged on El Alto above La Paz while the royalist troops were still campaigning in the surrounding provinces, trying to subdue the focal points of rebellion.[1] Fearing they would meet the same fate as residents of other besieged cities, the authorities in la Paz hastened to nip the problem in the bud by dislodging the Indians from their positions without delay. The rebels' large numerical superiority and the local soldiers' lack of professionalism prevented them from achieving this aim. Attacks on El Alto ended in disorganized retreats. Nor did the arrival of militia companies from Sorata and other nearby rural towns improve matters much: overwhelmed by the Indians' attacks, they abandoned the battlefield and fled back to the city. Dozens of creoles and mestizos lost their lives during these initial battles. In the early days of the siege, the Indians living in the suburban parishes of La Paz—the neighborhoods that lay outside its fortified city walls—often joined in with the attackers. Such was the case with the parish of San Sebastián, whose inhabitants went over to the rebel side, bringing with them all the cattle

---

1. Historical information and analysis in this section draw on Thomson 2002. The section is also based on Valle de Siles 1990; Fisher 1966; and Lewin 1957.

that the royalist troops had managed to commandeer on an incursion into Omasuyos province. The city dwellers would bitterly mourn this loss in the days to come. On March 26, Segurola launched one last attempt to expel the Indians from the highlands overlooking La Paz. Three columns carried out a coordinated attack on the enemy positions, each from a different flank. The result was as catastrophic as before: they lost more than thirty men, along with arms and munitions. The cavalry retreated at a gallop back to the city, and many soldiers, fearing the worst, sought refuge in the cathedral. The Indians got as far as the suburban parishes of Santa Bárbara, San Sebastián, and San Pedro, attacking their neighbors and setting fire to their houses. For several hours the La Paz residents were thrown into a state of utter panic. And though these battles caused more casualties among the Indians than among their enemies, it became evident that unless the regular Spanish army came to the rescue, the situation of the city was hopeless.

By late March, the noose had tightened around La Paz. The city's inhabitants lost all contact with the outside world. The insurgent forces, aware that regular troops dispatched from Buenos Aires and Tucumán would come to the city's rescue sooner or later, carried out attacks daily, descending to the city by day and climbing back up to El Alto by night. In many cases they used weapons that they had captured in battle. Though costly in lives—it is estimated that on a single day, March 28, the insurgents lost some 350 men—this constant harassment wrought a terrible psychological toll on the city's residents. Moreover, food soon began to run out. Keeping La Paz supplied with basic provisions rested more and more on making occasional and highly dangerous raids into the suburban neighborhoods. The rebels believed, with good reason, that it was only a matter of time before the city capitulated.

Around this time, Túpac Katari began an active correspondence with the archbishop of La Paz. At first, he limited himself to forwarding a letter from Túpac Amaru offering what Túpac Amaru used to offer— protection to any mestizos and creoles who would join the insurgent cause—and demanding that all others surrender. The archbishop warned him that he was caught in a horrible error and offered his services to attain a pardon for him from the highest authorities. Túpac Katari replied that the archbishop could ignore the high magistrates' judgments, since it was understood that Charles III of Spain had abdicated in favor of the new Inca king. He added that if all the corregidores (presumably including Segurola) were not turned over, the entire population of the city would be exterminated. He signed the letter, "I, the Viceroy Túpac Katari" (there was no need to specify for which king he served as viceroy). In late April, the Aymara leader exchanged letters along the same lines with Segurola. Katari tried to maintain the formalities appropriate for communications between military chiefs; Segurola treated him as an irrational creature.

On Friday, April 13, the Indians suddenly suspended their attacks. It was Good Friday, the beginning of one of the most important periods in the religious calendar for Andean communities. For several days, before the astonished gaze of the La Paz residents, they celebrated mass, drank, danced, and carried out a series of collective rituals. The religious rites were performed by Matías Borda, an Augustinian priest who had been held captive for several weeks in El Alto, and other clergymen who were similarly forced to offer their pastoral services. The insurgent forces were made up of thousands of indigenous families from several neighboring provinces. It was less an army than a community—many communities—in arms. Túpac Katari himself was accompanied by his wife, Bartolina Sisa, and his sister, Gregoria Apaza. Spanish sectors accused the Indians of falling back into ancient idolatries and atavistic beliefs, but nothing of the sort can be deduced from the eyewitness testimonies. The Aymara communities seem to have carried out their customary Easter religious celebrations. Like Indians in most of Peru, they practiced a form of Andean Catholicism that combined Christian elements with communal rituals dedicated to local deities and ancestor worship. This is what they had been doing for centuries, year after year, before the tolerant, resigned, or indifferent gaze of rural priests, nonindigenous townspeople, and colonial rulers. The war had changed only the perception of the Spanish groups, not the indigenous religious practices.

The truce lasted as long as the festivities did. Indeed, the end of Easter was followed by the most furious attack on the city to date. As one witness testified, on the night of April 25 the Indians descended the mountainsides, "some approaching with flaming torches, trying to set fire to the houses; others with picks, hoping to break holes in the walls or knock them down to get into [the city]; and most of them attacking with great screams and throwing of rocks, helped by many rifles, which they fired upon us with all the ardor and valor that can be imagined" (Ballivián y Roxas 1872: 37). Túpac Katari placed great expectations on this action. He looked on from the heights—together with his wife, Bartolina Sisa, and Matías Borda and other clergymen—as the city burst into flames and street fighting multiplied. For a moment, victory seemed at hand. But to his great regret, the residents managed to hold out while indigenous casualties remained as high as ever. "Demons," Katari called the Spaniards when reports of the battle began to arrive.

After this failure, the rebels lost faith in the efficacy of mass attacks. But they kept the cordon drawn tight. During May and June, the Indians regularly shelled the city with cannon fire and carried out constant incursions. Just when food was beginning to give out and the predicament of the inhabitants was turning desperate, the long-awaited arrival of the regular army, led by Lieutenant Colonel Ignacio Flores, finally took place. On July 1, after 109 uninterrupted days of siege, the insurgents were dislodged from El Alto. There were no large-scale battles, however, only skirmishes, for Túpac Katari had ordered his forces to retreat in orderly fashion as soon as the royal army approached La Paz. So the siege had not actually been defeated, but had reached a tense impasse.

When the Spanish troops marched into La Paz, the neighbors greeted them with great jubilation. The panorama they found there was bleak: the most vibrant city in the Andes at the time was surrounded by trenches, assailed by disease and hunger, largely reduced to ashes, and overwhelmed with corpses.

July brought some relief. Fresh supplies began coming into the city again, and sanitation improved, along with the morale of the residents. But that wouldn't last long. To begin with, the long-anticipated invasion of Upper Peru by Tupamarista forces from the north finally took place. Aware of the crucial significance of the battle for La Paz, Diego Cristóbal Túpac Amaru, leader of the rebellion since the death of José Gabriel, sent a large contingent to the region. From Azángaro, the new Tupamarista general headquarters, Andrés Túpac Amaru, Miguel Bastidas, and other relatives and colonels in the Quechua peasant army descended with their troops. They first marched on Sorata, capital of Larecaja province and the place where most of the creoles, Spaniards, and mestizos from the towns east of La Paz had congregated. They set up a cordon around the village and, displaying the high levels of sophistication the insurgency had achieved, Andrés Túpac Amaru ordered a dam built so that the town could be inundated when enough water had accumulated. After the torrent did flood Sorata, the insurgents entered en masse, seized the treasures from the church, and set fire to the building, which had become the main place of refuge. In the central plaza the Tupamarista forces slaughtered everyone they considered hostile, without regard to ethnic origin, age, or gender. Then they marched on to El Alto.

If the arrival of the Amarus in the region boded no good for the Spanish inhabitants, the situation became frankly desperate in early August when Ignacio Flores decided to return to Charcas, owing to the impossibility of keeping his army in the field because of hunger, illness, and, above all, lack of discipline. In particular, the militiamen from Cochabamba had mutinied and gone home without waiting for orders. The contrast with what had happened in the Cusco region is again clear. The military superiority of the Spanish regular detachments had allowed them to win some battles, but as they failed to receive from some peasants the support that they had enjoyed in their fight against Túpac Amaru, the war turned into a long, laborious slog. Fearing that the Aymara forces would decimate what remained of his army, Flores felt obliged to abandon the city in a hurry. He was even unable to carry away the wounded. On August 7, as soon as the army had withdrawn, El Alto was once more covered with insurgent troops. The second siege of La Paz had begun.

There would be a different insurgent high command this time. Andrés Túpac Amaru had arrived in El Alto after his victory in Sorata. He set up his general headquarters on Cerro Calvario, a mountain overlooking La Paz from the north, directly opposite Túpac Katari's base on Pampahasi, a flat hilltop just east of the city. The Amarus provided the insurgents with prestige, experience, and cunning. Yet relations between the Aymara and the Quechua commands were complicated from the outset. Andrés Túpac Amaru demanded the leadership of the movement, as might be expected: why else would they all be fighting to reinstate Inca rule? But declaring loyalty to a distant and rather abstract king whose presence was embodied in decrees and letters was one thing; deferring to his personal command, much less that of his heirs and relatives, was quite another. The Aymara communities of La Paz were not risking everything—lives, families, possessions—in order to subordinate themselves to outsiders. Besides, it is worth recalling that prior to the Spanish conquest the Aymara peoples had been subjugated by the Incas through force. For the eighteenth-century Cusco aristocracy the Inca civilization and the Andean civilization might have become one and the same. But the Indians on the other side of Lake Titicaca did not think that way. They had a different view of history. This may not have been the most pressing issue at a time of total war against a powerful common enemy. But it was still an issue. It was said, for instance, that while looking at the city in flames during the mass attack on April 25, Túpac Katari had muttered that now that La Paz had been conquered, they would have to wage war on the Amarus so that he could become the only monarch of these realms (Ballivián y Roxas 1872: 230).

Once the Quechua commanders from the north had established themselves in El Alto, these tensions quickly rose to the surface. During the early days of the second siege, as Katari openly resisted subordinating himself to the Cusco chiefs, the Amarus had him arrested and brought to their encampment. They soon realized, of course, that this situation was untenable: Katari exercised a powerful influence over the Aymara peasants, so he was irreplaceable, and their only chance for success lay in giving him all the help they could. Following a series of conversations, he was thus formally named commander of the siege of La Paz. Andrés Túpac Amaru and Miguel Bastidas held authority only over the Quechua troops. Though this arrangement seemed at last to stabilize relationships within the insurgent high command, Katari did not consider the book closed on the incident. It is very illustrative of his style of leadership that, soon afterward, he ordered the capture of the Tupamarista colonel who had arrested him. He then had the colonel hanged and quartered in El Alto.

For the residents of La Paz, the reinstatement of the siege meant the return of hunger and illness. Witnesses spoke of people forced to eat leather, tobacco pouches, cats, mules, and every animal they could find, alive or dead. Dogs were especially sought after: they were fat from eating the bodies that had been left piled up in the open air. At least two testimonies refer to cases of cannibalism. The other option was to risk leaving the fortified zone to eat wild plants. In early October, the residents discovered that an Indian market had been set up around the parish of San Pedro. A large number of people, tortured by hunger, ventured outside the city walls to buy provisions. But besides the exorbitant prices, they soon discovered that the insurgents took advantage of the situation to capture dozens of men and women. As the dead piled up, the cemetery was overwhelmed with corpses, and the stench became unbearable. The hospitals had to put as many as four patients to a bed; people were simply falling down dead in the streets. By the time the siege lifted, it is calculated that a third of the population of La Paz, some fifteen thousand people, had died from hunger, from illness, or at the hands of the rebels.

The second siege lasted more than two months, from early August until October 17, 1781. Its characteristics did not vary much from the first: constant harassment in the form of artillery shelling, stone throwing, rifle fire, and daily incursions into the city suburbs. Both Túpac Katari and Andrés Túpac Amaru kept communications open with the authorities and residents in La Paz. Túpac Katari repeatedly demanded freedom for his wife and top lieutenant, Bartolina Sisa, who had been captured in a skirmish. Both insisted that the creoles and mestizos would be pardoned if they agreed to put down their arms. Otherwise, they would meet the same fate as the Sorata dwellers. Indeed, Andrés Túpac Amaru designed a plan for flooding La Paz similar to the one he had used in the capital of Larecaja. In mid-September they began to build a dam at the head of the Choquepayu River in order to create an artificial lake large enough that the water would sweep away the city when they tore down the containing wall. This was a complex engineering project to which hundreds of workers were assigned. On the night of October 11, however, the dam gave way before it was ready. And though the water did sweep away several bridges and houses, causing great panic among the city's residents, the fortified trenches held up and the city suffered no greater damage. The failed attempt to flood La Paz turned out to be the last opportunity to force its surrender.

A few days later, on October 17, some eight thousand soldiers under lieutenant colonel José de Reseguín—the same army that had pacified the southern provinces—arrived in El Alto after fighting a series of battles and skirmishes with the rebel forces they had encountered on their way through the province of Sicasica. Faced with the imminent arrival of this powerful force, the insurgents fled their positions, as they had done in the first siege. But this time things would be different. After lifting the siege once and for all, the Spanish regular army immediately set out in pursuit of the Aymara forces and crushed them.

Túpac Katari sought refuge in the church of Peñas, a village north of La Paz where the Quechua troops and their leaders had dug in. He did not find the protection he sought there, however. By that time, the Tupamarista commanders were engaged in conversations with the Spanish authorities to end the rebellion. Negotiations had stepped up after the viceroy of Peru, Agustín de Jáuregui, at the suggestion of commander José del Valle, made a formal peace offer on September 12 in which he proclaimed a general amnesty for everyone who would put down their arms. Barely a week later, del Valle personally wrote a letter to Diego Cristóbal Túpac Amaru proposing a peace accord. He; his nephew Andrés Mendigure, the son of José Gabriel; Mariano Túpac Amaru; and all the leaders of the movement and all their followers would be pardoned. The proposal was tempting. After a full year of open warfare, considering the gloomy state of affairs both north and south of the Collao, the Tupamarista leaders must have begun to entertain serious doubts about their ability to defeat the royalist troops. The Amarus had proved quite successful in resisting assaults from the colonial armies and holding on to their control over vast rural areas of the Collao provinces. But they had been unable to expand the insurrection, and it could not possibly survive in isolation. On October 17, the same day Túpac Katari's forces were defeated in El Alto, Diego Cristóbal sent del Valle a letter accepting the general amnesty.

Therefore by the time Túpac Katari reached the village of Peñas, Túpac Amaru's principal heir had already dispatched instructions from Azángaro for his troops to surrender their weapons to Reseguín. Whereas the Amarus abided by the order, Katari instead retreated to Achacachi, a town on the eastern shore of Lake Titicaca, to try reorganizing the resistance. But it was too late for that. Between the military defeats in Cusco, La Paz, and Oruro, the campaigns of repression in Cochabamba, Lípez, and Porco, the collapse of the insurgency in Chayanta, and the armistice signed by the Amarus in southern Peru, the opportunity for rebellion had already passed. Even in highland provinces around La Paz, tens of thousands of Indians journeyed to Peñas to offer their surrender in exchange for a full pardon. Betrayed by one of his main collaborators, Túpac Katari was finally captured in early November.

The Aymara leader was led to a cell inside the church at Peñas. There he was summarily judged by Tadeo Diez de Medina, who was one of the most prominent residents of La Paz, a recently appointed minister of the Audiencia of Chile, and a judge advocate in the army. On November 14, Túpac Katari was tied to the tail of a horse and dragged through the streets to the town's main square. There he was drawn and quartered alive by four horses pulling on his arms and legs. His head was put on display soon afterward in the plaza of La Paz; the rest of his body parts were displayed in the pueblos of Ayoayo, Sicasica, Chulumani, Caquia-vari, and other rebel centers. The harsh sentence, Medina emphasized, was proportional to "the nature and quality of his crimes as a vile traitor, rebel, murderer, and fierce man or monster of humanity in his abominable and horrifying inclinations and customs" (Lewin 1957: 524).

16

....

The End of an Era

The Tupamarista revolution was a watershed in the history of the Andean peoples of Peru.[1] Until then the indigenous communities had been considered members of a republic, the "republic of Indians." It was a lesser republic, subordinated to the other one, the "republic of Spaniards," but a republic at last: a whole stratified society, with its small number of privileged people, its many commoners, its legal codes, its property systems, its religious practices, its languages, its historical memory. After the clamor for Inca restoration, the profaning of churches, and the slaughter of q'aras came to an end, the time-honored colonial model of "two republics" was gradually relegated to the past. The native peoples were increasingly seen as a class, or, rather, given the overlapping of economic and ethnic traits, as a caste. Their social practices and cultural beliefs were no longer understood as the idiosyncrasies of one of the many political entities that made up the baroque building of the Spanish monarchy. They now began to look like dead vestiges of a long-extinct civili-

1. Historical information and analysis in this section draw on Walker 1999; O'Phelan Godoy 1997; Campbell 1987; Sala i Vila 1996; Hünefeldt 1982; Platt 1982; Méndez 1995; Abercrombie 1998; Rowe 1954; and Larson 2004.

zation. The colonial elites, whether Peninsular or American, began to conceive of them as peasants, and acted accordingly.

Their main objective was to eradicate any symbolic representation associated with the Inca past and any preeminence extended to their putative descendants, the indigenous aristocracy. This change in government policy and social attitudes might have marked the most profound transformation in the modes of colonial domination since permanent institutions of Spanish rule had been established in the late sixteenth century. The new imperial policies, which were actively promoted by Visitor General General Antonio de Areche and the highest royal magistrates in Peru and Madrid, endeavored to root out the historical forces that had quietly led to the undermining of colonial hierarchies, the dilution of Indian subalternity, the creole elites' assumption of cultural Andean representations as their own, and the prominence of the Inca nobility. Thus paintings of Inca emperors were removed from public view, and the use of ancient Andean garb was forbidden. Theatrical representations of the Inca past and the conquest were banned, as was reading the seventeenth-century *Royal Commentaries of the Incas* by "El Inca" Garcilaso de la Vega. In his zeal to assimilate the Indians into the dominant culture and eliminate the long-standing multiculturalism of the Spanish monarchy, Areche even tried to stamp out the use of the native languages, Quechua and Aymara. He maintained in this regard that "it gives me the greatest sorrow to walk around this land not understanding those who speak to me, quite in spite of the frequency with which the king has ordered that they be taught, and that has not been sufficient" (quoted in Walker 2009). Reflecting on the deep causes of the revolution, Cusco's bishop, Juan Manuel de Moscoso, argued that the continuous display of "pagan" symbols had been "a major error" (Brading 1991: 491). Moscoso failed to mention that those symbols, besides being publicly exhibited, had not been considered merely "pagan" but part and parcel of the collective identity of Cusco society as a whole.

How did the Amarus adapt to this new climate? By early 1782, after complex negotiations, mutual accusations of betrayal, and a few skirmishes, all of Túpac Amaru's heirs had finally laid down their arms. Although a few isolated outbursts of violence still occurred from time to time in the southern Peruvian highlands and the Lake Titicaca region, for all practical purposes the Tupamarista uprising had ended. Nevertheless, the armistice was a product of necessity, not of conviction, and only served to postpone for a while the true policies of pacification. There would be no place for the Amarus in the new order of things. Fifteen months after the armistice, Crown magistrates in Peru invoking real facts (the Amarus had never condescended to repudiate their illustrious relative) and fake pretexts (alleged plots for a new uprising) declared that Diego Cristóbal and his family had broken the peace accords and therefore ordered their arrest. In April 1782, Diego Cristóbal, his mother, and several of his collaborators were executed in Cusco. The execution was even more brutal than that of Túpac Amaru himself. Andrés Mendigure and Mariano Túpac Amaru were shipped off to Spain; they died on the voyage. Even distant relatives who had not been involved in the rebellion were arrested and sent into exile. As soon as the colonial authorities felt confident that the risks of indigenous retaliation had vanished, they made it clear that figures such as the Amarus would no longer be tolerated anymore.

The demise of the Amarus is indicative of a larger phenomenon with profound and enduring consequences: the irreversible decline of the native chieftainships. All rebel caciques were stripped of their offices and titles, which were abolished; even those who had remained neutral became the objects of countless accusations and legal proceedings. It is true that some loyalist caciques were rewarded by the Crown, but the symbolic and material foundations of their former prominence had vanished. To survive, they had to disavow their past and their noble ancestry; the price of survival was their total Hispanicization. While their status had traditionally rested on their lineage (the Cusco nobles were willing to spend any amount of money and energy to prove their Inca blood, as Túpac Amaru's travails prior to the rebellion showed), it now came to depend on the degree of their cooperation with the downfall of those who had risen up in the name of their ancestors. Moreover, the caciques were deprived of one of the crucial prerogatives of the office: the collection of tribute. Without this power, the ethnic chiefs lost most of the access to the economic resources and labor force of the community. Stripped of both their economic privileges and the symbols of social prestige, the traditional colonial caciques went into an irreversible decline. They were replaced by indigenous officials elected by the community, such as the ones called *alcaldes varayocs*, and also by new "tribute-collector caciques," who for the most part were mestizos or creoles completely alien to the communities and discretionally appointed by the Spanish provincial governors.

The replacement of traditional caciques represented more than a mere change in authority figures; it was associated with transformations in the very nature of the rural community. The disappearance of the Andean lords and the rise of the alcaldes are said to have been accompanied "by the destructuring of the traditional ethnic ties that grouped the community members together horizontally" and to have constituted a process that was "democratizing yet at the same time disintegrative" (Hünefeldt 1982: 34–35). A form of sociability thus began to develop that was based less on kinship and sacred notions of community identity and history and more on "voluntary" ties typical of social groupings with a greater degree of ethnic and cultural fragmentation. To be sure, during the first decades of the independence era the Andean community continued to function as the main source of tribute and labor for the emerging national states and the rural elites. And, naturally, the rhythms and intensity of this transformation varied greatly from region to region: it was less marked in the highlands than in the valleys, in Bolivia than in Peru, in northern Potosí than in La Paz. It is not by chance that in the course of the nineteenth century, the province of Chayanta witnessed vigorous movements in defense of the territorial integrity of the ayllus, or that Bolivia rather than Peru served as the setting for a rebellion on a national scale with deep nativist roots such as the one led by Pablo Zárate Willka in 1899 (see Larson 2004: 231–242). In any event, by the time the Bolivian and Peruvian governments could diversify their sources of fiscal revenues (and thus depend less on Indian tribute), and the rise of export economies increased the value of land, and nineteenth-century liberal politicians set out to mount concerted assaults on the corporate organization of the indigenous community, the Andean peoples' ability to defend their traditional forms of social and political organization was severely hindered. Decades-old changes in the fabric of the indigenous community limited the natives' capacity to check the incursions of haciendas into communal land or the ideological and legal attacks on their very right to exist.

17

The Stubbornness of Facts

In the early 1810s, at a time when Napoleon was consolidating his control over the Iberian Peninsula and the Spanish monarchy was beginning to lose hold on its colonial empire, a creole-led rebellion broke out in Cusco. It was one of the revolts taking place across Spanish America as creole elites dealt with the effects of the liberal policies established by the Cortes of Cádiz in 1812. The Cortes—a parliamentary body composed of elected representatives from across Spain and Spanish America—was opposed to both the French occupation forces that controlled most of Spain outside of the southern port city of Cádiz and the absolutist regime that the Spanish Bourbons had imposed on its realms throughout the eighteenth century. The deliberations of the Cortes of Cádiz led to the approval of a constitution, which, for the first time in Spain's history, instituted a parliamentary monarchy. The viceroy of Peru, José Fernando de Abascal, a firm believer in absolutist rule, rejected any measure favoring regional autonomy or local representation in the government. He roundly refused to implement the Constitution of 1812 and ruthlessly repressed the Cusco creoles' armed movement.

Finding themselves hemmed in by royalist forces, the creole insurgents decided to appeal for military aid from Mateo García Pumacahua, the elderly cacique from the pueblo of Chinchero (Urubamba province) whom we saw three decades earlier leading his men against Túpac Amaru. Pumacahua had been one of the few members of the old Cusco aristocracy who, in recognition of his vital services to the Crown, managed to keep his privileges despite the implacable campaign of the colonial government to suppress the indigenous nobility and all cultural vestiges of the Inca past. Yet his attempts to assimilate into the provincial elite had not been trouble-free. As a reward for his military record, including not only his role in the events of 1780 but also in the repression of creole uprisings in the Upper Peru in 1809 and 1810, the cacique had been granted the military rank of colonel. He had also been named a member, and later president, of the Audiencia of Cusco, a tribunal created after the Tupamarista rebellion to expedite the administration of justice in the region. These were extraordinary appointments for someone of indigenous background. But precisely because many deemed the position inappropriate for someone of his ethnic origin, in 1812 he was removed from the presidency of the Audiencia. Feeling mistreated and humiliated, he wrote bitter letters to the viceroy complaining that there was no possible reason for his dismissal other than that he was an Indian. Having long since rejected eighteenth-century Inca nationalism, Pumacahua now decided to embrace creole nationalism instead. When the great landowners, merchants, lawyers, and other members of the Cusco elite once more saw a descendant of the Incas leading an army of Indians (and that these Indians sometimes referred to him as "the Inca"), they were deeply shaken. As the rebellion became radicalized, the insurgent creoles began to lose all the support of their peers. Pumacahua, left to his own devices, scored a few significant military victories such as seizing the cities of Puno and Arequipa, but eventually was defeated and captured, and in March 1815 he was executed.

Pumacahua had been one of the fiercest enemies of the Tupamarista movement. But in many ways his ideology is less significant than the symbolic foundations of his power and prominence. Put simply, Pumacahua sprang from the same civilization that had made the emergence of a figure like Túpac Amaru possible. It was a civilization in which the native imperial and cultural traditions were also the traditions and culture of Cusco society as a whole; in which the indigenous community—its systems of economic reciprocity, religious practices, government institutions, distribution of collective resources, and modes of participation in the regional markets—formed the core of the social experience of millions of Indians throughout the Andes. It is precisely the vitality of Andean society, and the vitality of the ties that bound Andean society to the world surrounding it, which indicate that the Tupamarista revolution stood for something more than a mere yearning for a return to former times. The rebels did not reject the political, economic, or religious institutions of their time altogether; rather, they reinterpreted them in the light of their own concepts. They had their own ideas of how the government, the justice system, and the market should work, what it meant to be a good Christian, and what it meant to be a subject of the king. They also had the political experience, mobilization skills, and self-reliance to attempt to put their beliefs into practice. They persuaded some creole and mestizo sectors as well. In the process, they radically subverted the place of the colonized peoples in the natural order of things: in other words, the view of cultural difference as a signifier of racial inferiority and the use of racial inferiority as a legitimate claim to rule. José Gabriel Condorcanqui Túpac Amaru was the most visible icon of this civilization; Mateo García Pumacahua, its last victim. In the times to come, the ruling elites of the new Andean countries might sometimes take pride in evoking the Inca past, but their conviction in the inherent unsuitability of present Indians to become full citizens never really wavered.

By the late twentieth century, to return to our point of departure, whereas the Bolivian and Peruvian states would construe the Tupamarista revolution as a harbinger of national independence, oppositional discourses of diverse ideological positions would turn it into the manifestation of transcendental Andean essentialisms. These are not errors of interpretation. For getting the history wrong—exalting what is, or what ought to be, and construing the past as origin and prefiguration—is a defining feature of political discourse. Historians are not necessarily any more correct, but they certainly are a little more scrupulous. Historians strive to analyze the past on its own terms, to scrutinize the paths not taken, the latent possibilities that time has turned into archaeological ruins: the worlds that might have been but were not.

GLOSSARY

ALCABALA

a royal tax on the sale of goods, levied on the seller and collected in customs houses (*aduanas*) at the entrances to towns and cities

AUDIENCIA

the highest court in colonial Spanish America administration; in the time period and area under study, the Audiencia of Lima had jurisdiction over Cusco and other provinces of the territory of modern Peru, and the Audiencia of Charcas over the provinces of Upper Peru (modern Bolivia)

AYLLU

Andean kin group that owns land collectively; the primary indigenous Andean social unit

CACIQUE

governor of an indigenous community; a member of the indigenous ruling nobility, also called ethnic authorities or ethnic lords

CHAPETÓN

greenhorn, newcomer; in colonial usage, a pejorative term for a Peninsular Spaniard

CHARCAS

the region surrounding Chuquisaca and under its immediate jurisdiction

CHOLO
a person of indigenous Andean ancestry who lives in the Spanish urban or mining world

CHUQUISACA
a city in Upper Peru (Bolivia) that served as seat of the Audiencia of Charcas; also known as Charcas or La Plata in colonial times, renamed Sucre after independence

COLLAO, THE
the high plateau (*altiplano*) region around Lake Titicaca, especially the portion of it that forms part of modern Peru

CORREGIDOR
the district governor or top Spanish official in a colonial province

CREOLE
criollo or *criolla*, a person born in Peru who traces his or her descent from Spain and who, in the colonial period, identifies culturally with Spain; compare Peninsular

CUSCO
the capital of the Inca empire until 1532 and a major provincial city in Spanish America thereafter; also spelled Cuzco

ETHNIC AUTHORITY, ETHNIC LORD
see cacique

HACIENDA
a large agricultural estate, typically owned by a wealthy creole and worked by Indian laborers, often growing crops for sale in nearby cities, towns, or mining centers

INCA
generally, the ruling lineage of the Cusco region that created the Inca empire and civilization; specifically, as "the Inca," the king or emperor of the Inca empire; also spelled Inka

GLOSSARY
....

MESTIZOS

people of mixed Spanish, Indian, and sometimes unacknowledged African ancestry

MITA

colonial institution of forced labor in the Andean region, especially the "Potosí mita," which forced each Andean pueblo from Cusco to southern Upper Peru to send one-seventh of its people to work in the mining center each year

NORTHERN POTOSÍ

a primarily Aymara-speaking cultural region in the central Bolivian highlands that corresponds to the colonial province Chayanta

PENINSULAR

a Spaniard from Spain; compare Creole

PUNA

the high grasslands ecosystem of the Andes, lying above the treeline (roughly 3,400 meters above sea level) and below the permanent snow line (roughly 4,500 meters above sea level)

REPARTO

forced sale of commodities at inflated prices, used by provincial corregidores to raise money from the Indian communities under their jurisdiction; also known as *repartimiento* or *reparto de mercancías*

SPANIARD, SPANISH

in colonial usage, these terms were used to describe creoles and Peninsulars alike

UPPER PERU

Alto Perú, the colonial jurisdiction of the Audiencia of Charcas, covering roughly the same area as modern Bolivia; see also Viceroyalty

VECINO

a non-Indian citizen of a city or town

VICEROYALTY

the highest level of government in colonial Spanish America; the viceregal court of Lima (established 1542) originally ruled all of Spanish South
America, but the Audiencia of Charcas (Upper Bolivia) was transferred to
the Viceroyalty of Río de la Plata when a new viceregal court was created
in Buenos Aires in 1776

REFERENCES

Abercrombie, Thomas. 1998. *Pathways of Memory and Power: Ethnography and History among an Andean People.* Madison: University of Wisconsin Press.

Adrián, Mónica. 1993. "Sociedad civil, clero y axiología oficial durante la rebelión de Chayanta: Una aproximación a partir de la actuación del cura doctrinero de San Pedro de Macha." *Boletín del Instituto de Historia Americana "Dr. E. Ravignani"* 8 (2): 29–54.

Aljovín de Losada, Cristóbal. 2005. "A Break with the Past? Santa Cruz and the Constitution." In *Political Cultures in the Andes, 1750–1950,* edited by Nils Jacobsen and Cristóbal Aljovín de Losada. Durham, NC: Duke University Press.

Amin, Shahid. 1995. *Event, Metaphor, Memory: Chauri Chaura 1922–1992.* New Delhi: Oxford University Press.

Andrade Padilla, Claudio. 1994. *La rebelión de Tomás Katari.* Sucre, Bolivia: CIPRES.

Arze, Silvia. 1991. "La rebelión de los ayllus de la provincia colonial de Chayanta (1777–1781)." *Estado y Sociedad* 8: 89–110.

Baker, Keith. 1990. *Inventing the French Revolution: Essays on French Political Culture in the Eighteenth Century.* Cambridge: Cambridge University Press.

Ballivián y Roxas, Vicente de. 1872. *Archivo boliviano: Colección de documentos relativos a la historia de Bolivia, durante la época colonial.* Paris: A. Franck.

Barragán, Rossana. 1999. *Indios, mujeres y ciudadanos: Legislación y ejercicio de la ciudadanía en Bolivia Siglo XIX.* La Paz: Fundación Diálogo.

Brading, David. 1991. *The First America: The Spanish Monarchy, Creole Patriotism, and the Liberal State, 1492–1867.* Cambridge: Cambridge University Press.

Burga, Manuel. 2005 [1988]. *Nacimiento de una utopía: Muerte y resurrección de los Incas.* 2nd ed. Lima: Universidad Nacional de San Marcos.

Cajías de la Vega, Fernando. 2004. *Oruro 1781: Sublevación de indios y rebelión criolla.* 2 vols. Lima: IFEA-IEB.

Cahill, David. 1990. "Taxonomy of a Colonial 'Riot': The Arequipa Disturbances of 1780." In *Reform and Insurrection in Bourbon New Granada and Peru*, edited by John Fisher, Allan Kuethe, and Anthony McFarlane. Baton Rouge: Louisiana University Press.

——. 1996. "Popular Religión and Appropiation: The Example of Corpus Christi in Eighteenth-Century Cuzco." *Latin American Research Review* 31, 67: 67–110.

——. 2003. "Una nobleza asediada. Los nobles incas del Cuzco en el ocaso colonial." In *Elites indígenas en los Andes. Nobles, caciques y cabildantes bajo el yugo colonial*, edited by David Cahill y Blanca Tovías. Quito: Ediciones Abya-Yala.

Campbell, Leon. 1987. "Ideology and Factionalism during the Great Rebellion, 1780–1782." In *Resistance, Rebellion, and Consciousness in the Andean Peasant World, 18th to 20th Centuries*, edited by Steve Stern. Madison: University of Wisconsin Press.

Chartier, Roger. 1991. *The Cultural Origins of the French Revolution*. Durham, NC: Duke University Press.

Clendinnen, Inga. 1987. *Ambivalent Conquest: Maya and Spaniard in Yucatan, 1517–1570*. Cambridge: Cambridge University Press.

Colección documental de la independencia del Perú. 1971. 10 vols. Lima: Comisión Nacional del Sesquicentenario de la Independencia del Perú.

Colección documental del bicentenario de la revolución emancipadora de Túpac Amaru. 1980, vols. 1–2. Lima: Comisión Nacional de la Revolución Emancipadora de Túpac Amaru.

Cornblit, Oscar. 1995. *Power and Violence in the Colonial City: Oruro from the Mining Renaissance to the Rebellion of Tupac Amaru (1740–1782)*. New York: Cambridge University Press.

Cornejo Bouroncle, Jorge. 1949. *Túpac Amaru: La revolución precursora de la emancipación continental*. Cusco: Universidad Nacional de Cuzco.

da Costa, Emilia Viotti. 1994. *Crowns of Glory, Tears of Blood: The Demerara Slave Rebellion of 1823*. Oxford: Oxford University Press.

Deans-Smith, Susan, and Gilbert M. Joseph, eds. 1999. *Hispanic American Historical Review* 79, special issue titled "Mexico's New Cultural History: ¿Una Lucha Libre?"

de la Fuente, Ariel. 2000. *Children of Facundo: Caudillo and Gaucho Insurgency during the Argentine State-Formation Process (La Rioja, 1853–1870)*. Durham, NC: Duke University Press.

Di Meglio, Gabriel. 2007 *¡Viva el bajo pueblo! La plebe urbana de Buenos Aires y la política entre la Revolución de Mayo y el rosismo (1810–1829)*. Buenos Aires: Prometeo.

Estenssoro Fuchs, Juan Carlos. 2003. *Del paganismo a la santidad: La incorporación de los indios del Perú al catolicismo, 1532–1750*. Translated by Gabriela Ramos. Lima: IFEA.

Farge, Arlette. 1992. *Subversive Words: Public Opinion in Eighteenth-Century France.* University Park: Pennsylvania State University Press.

Fisher, John, Allan Kuethe, and Anthony McFarlane, eds. 1990. *Reform and Insurrection in Bourbon New Granada and Peru.* Baton Rouge: Louisiana State University Press.

Fisher, Lillian E. 1966. *The Last Inca Revolt, 1780–1783.* Norman: University of Oklahoma Press.

Flores Galindo, Alberto, ed. 1976. *Túpac Amaru II—1780.* Lima: Retablo de Papel Ediciones.

———. 2010 [1987]. *In Search of an Inca: Identity and Utopia in the Andes,* edited and translated by Carlos Aguirre, Charles Walker, and Willie Hiatt. Cambridge: Cambridge University Press.

Garrett, David. 2003. "Los incas borbónicos: La élite indígena en vísperas de Tupac Amaru." *Revista andina* 36: 9–64.

———. 2005. *Shadows of Empire: The Indian Nobility of Cusco, 1750–1825.* Cambridge: Cambridge University Press.

Geertz, Clifford. 1973. *The Interpretation of Cultures.* New York: Basic Books.

Ginzburg, Carlo. 1992. *The Cheese and the Worms: The Cosmos of a Sixteenth Century Miller.* Translated by John and Anne Tedeschi. Baltimore: Johns Hopkins University Press.

Glave, Luis Miguel. 1989. *Trajinantes: Caminos indígenas en la sociedad colonial siglos XVI–XVII.* Lima: Instituto de Apoyo Agrario.

———. 1990. "Sociedad campesina y violencia rural en el escenario de la gran rebelión indígena de 1780." *Histórica* 14 (1): 27–68.

———. 1999. "The 'Republic of Indians' in Revolt (c. 1680–c. 1790)." In *The Cambridge History of the Native Peoples of the Americas,* vol. 3, edited by Frank Salomon and Stuart Schwartz. Cambridge: Cambridge University Press.

Glave, Luis Miguel, and María Isabel Remy. 1983. *Estructura agraria y vida rural en una región andina: Ollantaytambo entre los siglos XVI y XIX.* Cusco: Centro de Estudios Bartolomé de las Casas.

Golte, Jürgen. 1980. *Repartos y rebeliones: Túpac Amaru y las contradicciones de la economía colonial.* Lima: IEP.

Greenblatt, Stephen, ed. 1993. *New World Encounters.* Berkeley: University of California Press.

Gruzinski, Serge. 1993. *The Conquest of Mexico: The Incorporation of Indian Societies into the Western World, 16th–18th Centuries.* Translated by Eileen Corrigan. New York: Polity.

Guardino, Peter. 1996. *Peasants, Politics and the Formation of Mexico's National State: Guerrero, 1800–1857.* Stanford, CA: Stanford University Press.

———. 2005. *The Time of Liberty: Popular Culture in Oaxaca, 1750–1850.* Durham, NC: Duke University Press.

Guha, Ranajit. 1983. *Elementary Aspects of Peasant Insurgency in Colonial India.* Oxford: Oxford University Press.

Guha, Ranajit, and Gayatri Chakravorty Spivak, eds. 1988. *Selected Subaltern Studies.* New York: Oxford University Press.

Halperín Donghi, Tulio. 1975. *Politics, Economics and Society in Argentina in the Revolutionary Period.* Translated by Richard Southern. Cambridge: Cambridge University Press.

Hidalgo Lehuede, Jorge. 1983. "Amarus y cataris: Aspectos mesiánicos de la rebelión indígena de 1781 en Cusco, Chayanta, La Paz y Arica." *Revista Chungara* 10: 117–138.

Hobsbawm, Eric. 1973. "Peasant Politics." *Journal of Peasant Studies* 1: 3–22.

Hünefeldt, Christine. 1982. *Lucha por la tierra y protesta indígena: Las comunidades indígenas del Perú entre colonia y república.* Bonn: Bonner Americanische Studien.

Hunt, Lynn. 1984. *Politics, Culture, and Class in the French Revolution.* Berkeley: University of California Press.

James, C. L. R. 1963. *The Black Jacobins: Toussaint L'Ouverture and the San Domingo Revolution.* New York: Vintage Books.

Joseph, Gilbert M., ed. 2001. *Reclaiming the Political in Latin American History: Essays from the North.* Durham, NC: Duke University Press.

Klein, Herbert. 1993. *Haciendas and Ayllus: Rural Society in the Bolivian Andes in the Eighteenth and Nineteenth Centuries.* Stanford, CA: Stanford University Press.

Knight, Alan. 2002. "Subalterns, Signifiers, and Statistics: Perspectives on Mexican Historiography." *Latin American Research Review* 37: 136–158.

Larson, Brooke. 1988. *Colonialism and Agrarian Transformation in Bolivia: Cochabamba, 1550–1900.* Princeton, NJ: Princeton University Press.

———. 2004. *Trials of Nation Making: Liberalism, Race, and Ethnicity in the Andes, 1810–1910.* New York: Cambridge University Press.

Lasso, Marixa. 2007. *Myths of Harmony: Race and Republicanism during the Age of Revolution, Colombia 1795–1831.* Pittsburgh: University of Pittsburgh Press.

Levi, Giovanni. 1988. *Inheriting Power: The Story of an Exorcist.* Translated by Lydia G. Cochrane. Chicago: University of Chicago Press.

Lewin, Boleslao. 1957. *La rebelión de Túpac Amaru y los orígenes de la emancipación americana.* Buenos Aires: Hachette.

Mallon, Florencia. 1994. "The Promise and Dilemma of Subaltern Studies: Perspectives from Latin American History." *American Historical Review* 99: 1491–1515.

———. 1995. *Peasant and Nation: The Making of Postcolonial Mexico and Peru.* Berkeley: University of California Press.

Markham, Clements. 1910. *The Incas of Peru*. London: Smith, Elder, & Co.

Méndez, Cecilia. 1995. *Incas sí, indios no: Apuntes para el estudio del nacionalismo criollo en el Perú*. Lima: IEP.

——. 2001. "The Power of Naming, or the Construction of Ethnic and National Identities in Peru: Myth, History and the Iquichanos." *Past and Present* 171: 127–160.

——. 2005. *The Plebeian Republic: The Huanta Rebellion and the Making of the Peruvian State, 1820–1850*. Durham, NC: Duke University Press.

Mignolo, Walter D. 1997. *The Darker Side of the Renaissance: Literacy, Territoriality, and Colonization*. Ann Arbor: University of Michigan Press.

Moreno Cebrián, Alfredo. 1977. *El corregidor de Indios y la economía peruana del siglo XVIII: Los repartos forzosos de mercancías*. Madrid: Instituto González Fernández de Oviedo.

Moreno Yáñez, Segundo. 1977. *Sublevaciones indígenas en la Audiencia de Quito: Desde comienzos del siglo XVIII hasta finales de la colonia*. Quito: Pontífica Universidad Católica del Ecuador.

Murra, John. 1975. *Formaciones económicas y políticas del mundo andino*. Lima: IEP.

Neruda, Pablo. 1991 [1950]. *Canto General*. Translated by Jack Schmitt. Berkeley: University of California Press.

O'Phelan Godoy, Scarlett. 1985. *Rebellions and Revolts in Eighteenth Century Peru and Upper Peru*. Cologne: Böhlau.

——. 1995. *La gran rebelión en los Andes: De Túpac Amaru a Túpac Catari*. Cusco: Centro Bartolomé de las Casas.

——. 1997. *Kurakas sin sucesiones: Del cacique al alcalde de indios (Perú y Bolivia 1750–1835)*. Cusco: Centro Bartolomé de las Casas.

Ossio, Juan M., ed. 1973. *Ideología mesiánica del mundo andino*. Lima: Ignacio Prado Pastor.

Ozouf, Mona. 1991. *Festivals and the French Revolution*. Cambridge, MA: Harvard University Press.

Pease, Franklin. 1973. *El dios creador andino*. Lima: Mosca Azul.

Penry, Elizabeth. 2006. "El discurso político indígena en Charcas colonial." *Anuario de Estudios Bolivianos, Archivísticos y Bibliográficos*.

Phelan, John Leddy. 1978. *The People and the King: The Comunero Revolution in Colombia, 1781*. Madison: University of Wisconsin Press.

Platt, Tristan. 1982. *Estado boliviano y ayllu andino: Tierra y tributo en el norte de Potosí*. Lima: IEP.

Rama, Ángel. 1996. *The Lettered City*. Translated by John Chastain. Durham, NC: Duke University Press.

Ramos, Gabriela. 1992. "Política eclesiástica y extirpación de idolatrías: Discursos y silencios en torno al Taqui Onqoy." *Revista Andina* 10: 147–69.

Rasnake, Roger. 1988. *Domination and Resistance: Authority and Power among an Andean People.* Durham, NC: Duke University Press.

Renan, Ernest. 1995 [1882]. "What Is a Nation?" In *The Nationalism Reader,* edited by Omar Dahbour and Micheline R. Ishay. Atlantic Highlands, NJ: Humanities Press.

Rivera Cusicanqui, Silvia. 1992. *Ayllus y proyectos de desarrollo en el norte de Potosí.* La Paz: Ediciones Aruwiyiri.

Rivera Cusicanqui, Silvia, and Rossana Barragán. 1997. "Presentación." In *Debates post coloniales: Una introducción a los estudios de la subalternidad,* edited by Rivera Cusicanqui y Barragán. La Paz: Ediciones Aruwiyiri.

Robins, Nicholas A. 2002. *Genocide and Millennialism in Upper Peru: The Great Rebellion of 1780–1782.* Westport, CT: Praeger.

Rowe, John. 1954. "El movimiento nacional inca del siglo XVIII." *Revista Universitaria* (Cuzco) 107: 17–47.

Saignes, Thierry. 1987. "De la borrachera al retrato: Los caciques de Charcas entre dos legitimidades." *Revista Andina* 5: 139–170.

———. 1995. "Indian Migration and Social Change in Seventeenth-Century Charcas." In *Ethnicity, Markets, and Migration in the Andes: At the Crossroads of History and Anthropology,* edited by Brooke Larson and Olivia Harris with Enrique Tandeter. Durham, NC: Duke University Press.

Sala i Vila, Núria. 1996. *Y se armó el tole tole: Tributos indígenas y movimientos sociales en el virreinato del Perú, 1784–1814.* Cusco: IER.

Sánchez-Albornoz, Nicolás. 1978. *Indios y tributos en el Alto Perú.* Lima: IEP.

Sandoval, Pablo, ed. 2009. *Repensando la subalternidad: Miradas críticas desde/sobre América Latina.* Lima: IEP-SEPHIS.

Scott, James C. 1985. *Weapons of the Weak: Everyday Forms of Peasant Resistance.* New Haven, CT: Yale University Press.

———. 1990. *Domination and the Arts of Resistance: Hidden Transcripts.* New Haven, CT: Yale University Press.

Serulnikov, Sergio. 2003. *Subverting Colonial Authority: Challenges to Spanish Rule in Eighteenth-Century Southern Andes.* Durham, NC: Duke University Press.

———. 2006. *Conflictos sociales e insurgencia en el mundo colonial andino: El norte de Potosí, siglo XVIII.* Buenos Aires: Fondo de Cultura Económica.

Spalding, Karen. 1984. *Huarochirí: An Andean Society under Inca and Spanish Rule.* Stanford, CA: Stanford University Press.

Stavig, Ward. 1999. *The World of Túpac Amaru: Conflict, Community, and Identity in Colonial Peru.* Lincoln: University of Nebraska Press.

Stern, Steve, ed. 1987. *Resistance, Rebellion, and Consciousness in the Andean Peasant World, 18th to 20th Centuries.* Madison: University of Wisconsin Press.

———. 1987. "The Age of the Andean Insurrection, 1742–1782: A Reappraisal." In

Resistance, Rebellion, and Consciousness in the Andean Peasant World, 18th to 20th Centuries, edited by Steve Stern. Madison: University of Wisconsin Press.

Stone, Lawrence. 1979. "The Revival of Narrative: Reflections on a New Old History." *Past and Present* 85: 3–24.

Szeminski, Jan. 1984. *La utopía tupamarista*. Lima: Pontífica Universidad Católica.

——. 1987. "Why Kill the Spaniards? New Perspectives on Andean Insurrectionary Ideology in the 18th Century." In *Resistance, Rebellion, and Consciousness in the Andean Peasant World, 18th to 20th Centuries*, edited by Steve Stern. Madison: University of Wisconsin Press.

Tandeter, Enrique. 1992. *Coacción y mercado: La minería de la plata en el Potosí colonial, 1692–1826*. Cusco: Centro Bartolomé de las Casas.

Taylor, William B. 1979. *Drinking, Homicide, and Rebellion in Colonial Mexican Villages*. Stanford, CA: Stanford University Press.

Thompson, E. P. 1975. *Whigs and Hunters: The Origin of the Black Act*. New York: Pantheon Books.

——. 1991. *Customs in Common: Studies in Traditional Popular Culture*. London: Merlin.

Thomson, Sinclair. 2002. *We Alone Will Rule: Native Andean Politics in the Age of Insurgency*. Madison: University of Wisconsin Press.

Thurner, Mark. 1997. *From Two Republics to One Divided: Contradicting Postcolonial Nation Making in Andean Peru*. Durham, NC: Duke University Press.

Tilly, Charles. 1978. *From Mobilization to Revolution*. Reading, PA: Addison-Wesley.

——. 1986. *The Contentious French*. Cambridge, MA: Harvard University Press.

Todorov, Tzvetan. 1992. *The Conquest of America: The Question of the Other*. Translated by Richard Howard. New York: Harper Perennial.

Valcárcel, Carlos Daniel. 1977. *Túpac Amaru, precursor de la independencia*. Lima: Universidad Nacional Mayor de San Marcos.

Valle de Siles, María Eugenia. 1990. *Historia de la rebelión de Túpac Catari, 1781–1782*. La Paz: Editorial Don Bosco.

Van Young, Eric. 2001. *The Other Rebellion: Popular Violence, Ideology, and the Mexican Struggle for Independence, 1810–1821*. Stanford, CA: Stanford University Press.

Vega, Garcilaso de la. 1966 [1609–1617]. *Royal Commentaries of the Incas, and General History of Peru*. Translated by Harold Livermore. Austin: University of Texas Press.

Wachtel, Nathan. 1976. *Los vencidos: Los indios del Perú frente a la conquista española (1532–1570)*. Madrid: Alianza Editorial.

Walker, Charles, ed. 1996. *Entre la retórica y la insurgencia: Las ideas y los movimientos sociales en los Andes, Siglo XVIII*. Cusco: Centro Bartolomé de las Casas.

——. 1999. *Smoldering Ashes: Cuzco and the Creation of Republican Peru, 1780–1840*. Durham, NC: Duke University Press.

———. 2008. "Introduction." In *The Tupac Amaru and Catarista Rebellions: An Anthology of Sources*, edited and translated by Ward Stavig and Ella Schmidt. Indianapolis, IN: Hackett.

———. 2009. "The Indulto and Its Malcontents: Spanish Divisions and the Tupac Amaru Rebellion." Paper presented at the Latin American Studies Association annual meeting, Rio de Janeiro, June 2009.

Womack, John. 1969. *Zapata and the Mexican Revolution*. New York: Vintage Books.

Zuidema, R. Tom. 1990. *Inca Civilization in Cuzco*. Translated by Jean-Jacques Decoster. Austin: University of Texas Press.

INDEX

Abercrombie, Thomas, 135

Acasio (Chayanta province), 58

Agriculture, Andean, 18, 21; changes in, 118. *See also* Haciendas

Alcaldes, 66, 74–75, 81, 85, 87, 137–38

Alós, Joaquín, 19, 24, 26–34, 37–38, 55, 57, 61, 77

Álvarez Villarroel, Manuel, 62, 65

Andean Catholicism, 21, 39, 62, 93, 127

Andean rural social organization, 18, 22–23, 137–38

"Andean utopia," xiv, 8–10, 68, 118–19

Apaza, Julián. *See* Tupac Katari

Areche, Antonio de, 24, 101–8, 111–12, 136

Arequipa, 1, 2, 42, 140

Arque (Cochabamba province), 92, 93

Arriaga, Antonio de, 35–38, 43–45, 101–2, 107

Audiencia of Charcas, 17, 19, 23–26, 33, 62, 75, 143

Audiencia of Cusco, 140

Audiencia of Lima, 106, 143

Aullagas (Chayanta province), 62, 65

Auquimarca (ethnic group), 95

Ayaviri Cuisara family, 58

Ayllus, 18, 20, 28, 118, 138, 143

Ayoayo (Sicasica province), 116, 133

Azángaro (town, province), 2, 46, 108, 110, 112, 121, 128, 132

Bastidas, Micaela, xii–xiii, 46–47, 99–100, 104–7, 112

Bastidas, Miguel, 100, 107, 112, 128, 130

Bernal, Blas, 24, 28

Betancour, Diego Felipe, 36

Bodega y Llano, Manuel de la, 60, 66–67, 73–75, 77

Bodies of enemies, treatment of, 62, 83, 87, 89, 93–96, 106, 123, 130, 133

Bourbon Reforms, xiv–xv, 21, 24, 42, 48, 103, 139

Buenos Aires, xi, xii, 2, 25–26, 37, 42, 76, 79, 89, 146

Burga, Manuel, 8–9

Caciques, xi, xii, 2, 19, 40–41, 52–53, 76, 140, 144; declining legitimacy of, 20–21, 23–24, 37–38, 118; as